D1639413

00301188159

GIANTS *of* ASIA

WHAT THE
UNITED NATIONS
IS REALLY LIKE:
THE VIEW
FROM
THE TOP

conversations with

BAN KI-MOON

TOM PLATE

Marshall Cavendish
Editions

© 2012 Thomas Gordon Plate

Research by Yena Kim and Esther Joe. Photographs courtesy of Tom Plate and Esther Joe.

Project editor: Lee Mei Lin
Design by Bernard Go Kwang Meng
Cover illustration by P.K. Cheng

Published by Marshall Cavendish Editions
An imprint of Marshall Cavendish International
1 New Industrial Road, Singapore 536196

Other Marshall Cavendish Offices
Marshall Cavendish Corporation. 99 White Plains Road, Tarrytown NY 10591-9001, USA • Marshall Cavendish International (Thailand) Co Ltd. 253 Asoke, 12th Flr, Sukhumvit 21 Road, Klongtoey Nua, Wattana, Bangkok 10110, Thailand • Marshall Cavendish (Malaysia) Sdn Bhd, Times Subang, Lot 46, Subang Hi-Tech Industrial Park, Batu Tiga, 40000 Shah Alam, Selangor Darul Ehsan, Malaysia.

Marshall Cavendish is a trademark of Times Publishing Limited

National Library Board Singapore Cataloguing in Publication Data
Plate, Tom.
Conversations with Ban Ki-Moon : what the United Nations is really like : the view from the top / Tom Plate. – Singapore : Marshall Cavendish Editions, c2012.
p. cm.
Includes bibliographical references.
ISBN : 978-981-4302-04-3

1. Pan, Ki-mun, 1944- - Interviews. 2. United Nations. – Secretary-General - Interviews.
3. Statesman – Korea (South) - Interviews. 4. Diplomats – Korea (South) – Interviews.
I. Title. II. Series: Giants of Asia.

D863.7.P36
341.23092 — dc23   OCN798530708

Printed in Singapore by KWF Printing Pte Ltd

To

Ashley Alexandra Jones

She is my warm and bright and utterly charming daughter,
our only child, now an accomplished student at
Loyola Marymount University in Los Angeles,
and future teacher of public school students.
They will be very lucky indeed.

I have always especially appreciated that
she understands her father so very well.

A Note on the Conversations

MUCH OF THE dialogue with Ban Ki-moon emerged in the relatively serene setting of the north end of the reception room of his official residence in New York City, and is largely put into that setting. In that room we had over many months seven uninterrupted two-hour sessions coming to an end in March 2012. This was then the very beginning of his second term. But there were also a half-dozen informal exchanges, in various dining or entertainment venues around Manhattan, and almost always with Mrs. Ban (Yoo Soon-taek). These will appear in spots, integrated when possible with the theme under discussion.

The *Giants of Asia* series, of which this book is the fourth, aims at ease of reading and understanding, so herewith a transcribing note: In his spoken English on complex issues, the former foreign minister of South Korea understandably tends to slip into Korean-like grammatical constructions, with pronunciations that are not difficult to understand face to face — but when transcribed exactly as spoken can make for bumpy reading — and can convey the impression of an imprecise mind. With Ban, intellectual looseness is rare, though deliberate ambiguity is not. And so for the sake of clarity and ease of understanding, I have edited the conversations from a kind of Korean-construction English into a normal-appearing universal English. To have done otherwise would not only have made the conversations difficult to follow but would have only served to mislead the reader. (For the historical record, the interviews in the official UNSG residence are all on audio digital; the vast majority of them are on digital video as well.)

As with the prior books in *Giants of Asia* — on Singapore's Lee Kuan Yew, on Malaysia's Mahathir Mohamad, and on Thailand's Thaksin Shinawatra — an exceptional degree of cooperation and patience, not to mention frankness, is required by the principal subject of the book if its somewhat intimate and detailed "conversations" methodology is to provide true value. In Ban Ki-moon's case, no one could have been more patient, or offered more quality time, or been more personally gracious. But unlike the prior three giants of Asia interviewed by me, Ban remains in active high office at the very time of these conversations — and was constantly under tremendous political and diplomatic pressures. This made for significant differences for this book, as you will see.

Tom Plate
Beverly Hills, California
September 2012

Contents

PREFACE • 9

OUR WORLD TODAY USING
TWO DIFFERENT PERSPECTIVES • 12

Weekend Plans • 14

Secret diary? ... Pakistan connection ... no call waiting ...
sanity questions ... economy travel ... UN first lady
Conversations with Mrs. Ban

The Korean Connection • 57

The quiet Confucian ... future foreign minister ...
getting sacked ... Powell telephones
Harvard professors on Ban Ki-moon

Asian Workaholic • 85

No respect ... power not eternal ... how they lie ... Ban and Israel

The Mandela Marker • 117

Global not local ... R2P ... beyond national interest ... UN staff ...
natural evolution of history ... golden parachute for tyrants?

Women and Ban • 141
Looking down at their shoes …
not a utopian world … isn't it a pity?

The Bosses of All Bosses • 162
The Fab Five … bit of Bolton … the beginning of trouble …
unjust to Japan ... happy trickster ... step up, Korea and China

Parting Dreams • 194
Shrinking turtle … cat and canary … slippery deal seal

A Utopian Goodbye • 224

WORKS CONSULTED AND RECOMMENDED • 235

THANKING THOSE WHO
HELPED MAKE THIS BOOK POSSIBLE • 237

ABOUT THE AUTHOR • 239

Ban Ki-moon and the author at the official residence
of the UN Secretary General in New York (March 2012)

Preface

I WAS JUST 20 years of age when I walked boldly into the United Nations Secretariat for the first time, full of idealism and ambition. This is the towering building adjacent to the East River on the edge of Manhattan, right near the tame eastern end of famous 42nd Street. I was looking for any UN job ... but *only* a UN job. I was desperate to work there. Like many Americans back then, and perhaps even now, I thought the UN an essential bridge to a more peaceful and less unjust world. How could I be part of it? Even a very small part...

And then, decades later, in the summer of 2006, I am a journalist writing columns about Asia from Los Angeles, and I get invited to lunch with a man who is also job hunting at the UN.

He was Ban Ki-moon, the foreign minister of the Republic of Korea, representing the southern and prosperous portion of the divided Korean Peninsula. His campaign staff had arranged — facing a long layover for a flight to Latin America, where he would troll for votes to support his candidacy — for us to meet at a hotel not far from the Los Angeles airport for "an exchange of views." But as we finished a session of almost two hours, he asked me, point-blank, in all earnestness: "I hope you can endorse my candidacy in your column."

Believe it or not, I actually asked him why anyone would ever want the job! So many people have come to dismiss the UN as hopelessly sunk in contradiction and ineffective paralysis. The job itself seemed impossible. His answer was plain-spoken but seemingly from the heart: He thought the UN could still help make the world a more peaceful and just place. At the least he wanted to give it a try. As it was Asia's turn to have one of theirs at the top of the UN — for only the second time in its history — he intended to campaign for it like there was no tomorrow.

Well, guess what happened? As fate would have it, we both wound up working at the UN — though in dramatically different capacities. In fact, four decades earlier, I had managed to land a junior statistical clerical job in the Secretariat — possibly one of the lowest possible positions in the worldwide UN system of many thousands of jobs. A year later I went back to college, having loved the experience. But he 'got hired' as secretary general of the entire United Nations — unquestionably the top job possible among some 63,000 or so worldwide, of which almost 8,000 are at the UN headquarters alone. All of the UN staff report, one way or the other, to the secretary general.

The story of these roughly parallel but very different lines (one trivial, one titanic) might have ended right there, except for one thing: The two lines recently intersected. Not long after his installation as the successor to Kofi Annan, sitting with him and his wife Yoo Soon-taek for tea at the official home provided for an incumbent UN secretary general, I asked if he would cooperate as the subject of a *Giants of Asia* book. He asked who else would be in the series and when I said the first one would be conversations with Lee Kuan Yew, the founding prime minister of Singapore, he responded by saying that was an excellent choice. I then said that as he was to be only the second SG in UN history to come from Asia, how could he not be a suitable subject for this series?

Ban Ki-moon said nothing at first, but then, deferentially gazed over to Soon-taek. There was a short but profound silence, and when his wife, after thinking for a few moments, returned his gaze with a slight nod, the UNSG looked at me and said decisively: "Okay, but I have never done anything like this before."

So this is how the book came to be.

Our World Today
Using Two Very Different Perspectives

On the one hand:
THE GARDEN
from 'UTOPIA'
— *the classic by Sir Thomas More, 1516*

"The many great gardens of the world, of literature and poetry, of painting and music, of religion and architecture, all make the point as clear as possible: The soul cannot thrive in the absence of a garden. If you don't want paradise, you are not human; and if you are not human, you don't have a soul."

On the other:
THE JUNGLE
from 'LEVIATHAN'
— the classic by Thomas Hobbes, 1651

"To this war of every man against every man ... Where there is no common power, there is no law, where no law, no injustice. Force, and fraud, are in war the cardinal virtues. ... No arts; no letters; no society; and which is worst of all, continual fear, and danger of violent death: and the life of man, solitary, poor, nasty, brutish and short."

Weekend Plans

Secret diary? … Pakistan connection … no call waiting … sanity questions … economy travel … UN first lady

IT IS GETTING near the end of a brutal backbreaking day, about 6pm on a Thursday in Manhattan. Ban Ki-moon trudges up the stairs of the townhouse that is the official residence of the secretary general of the United Nations. *Plunk … plunk …* step by step, up to the second floor. Each step … slow, careful, almost plotted, as if trying to avoid slips but determined to get to the top, though as noiselessly as possible.

Over time one will sense the sincere desire of this UN secretary general not to keep people waiting, much less make a slip up, whether on the home staircase or the much trickier inclines of international politics.

You think: He just has to be looking forward to the weekend collapse, as most mortals do. But this will be proven dead wrong. He doesn't collapse, this weekend or any other. He just keeps going and going … and going. You'll see. It is almost bizarre.

For about half an hour I wait for him, but this is no big deal. Journalists are accustomed to waits. We welcome them. They give us more time to think about our questions — and to snoop around.

And perhaps make the subject feel guilty for being late — perhaps even creating exploitable guilt, the journalist's favorite.

Let's survey the expanse of the second-floor of this official UN residence. It's a classy joint. The library room next door is dark and woody, if a bit stuffy for my taste, and the other room, smaller but much brighter, spotlights a fireplace and a desk underneath a bluish map of the world. It's for The Man, obviously, but it looks too tidy, as if hardly ever used. Must be a photo-op desk.

Back to the fairly bright reception room, where our conversations are to be held — neat pictures of Ban and various VIPs, a corner piano (with family pictures on the mantel, three children, wife) and assorted furniture obviously not purchased from the average discount warehouse. Elegant and warm, not too stuffy.

The townhouse has four stories and, at prestigious #3 Sutton Place, sits amid a neighborhood that is almost quiet for madhouse Manhattan. It is laid out as if in a back-to-the-future fashion of the carriage-drawn 19th century. The main pattern is of tidy crossword puzzles of low-rise 19th-century townhomes as well as formidable co-op apartment buildings, the former with graceful façades smiling over tree-lined streets or, to the rear, the East River, the latter with white-gloved doormen looking wearily pretentious.

This is no gaudy neighborhood like the East Village but a fancy address, and a substantial place of residence for the international law-firm partner, the famous book publisher, the world diplomat — whether Henry Kissinger (he's on 52nd Street) or, well, Ban Ki-moon (on 57th).

Certainly the neighbors need have no worries about the wild or the unruly taking over. On that score they have little to fear from having the Bans next door. As for the New York Police Department kiosk planted outside on the corner curb: I have never seen any officer in it. Maybe the cute kiosk is all that's needed to deter the terrorist.

The Bans are perfect for this neighborhood in which the permanent UN residence has placed them. I am to learn that, notwithstanding the significance of the job he holds and all the official hoopla around it, Ki-moon and his wife Soon-taek are the quietest couple. They go to parties when invited, but they rarely give them. They don't go out at night, except for official functions when formally invited. He's not home all that much, anyhow; and, given the choice, she'd rather seek out a dark movie house than stand under the bright lights.

Ban hits the top of the staircase and leans in as if peeking in, a little sheepishly. He stands about 5 feet 10 inches tall (and weighs in — I am told — at a very trim 168 pounds) and wears a plain gray suit, a nice smile under nondescript wire-rimmed glasses and a lined face that's maybe trying to cover up flecks of annoyance, like a secret UN document.

Bad day at the office?

He doesn't say anything except 'good to see you again', warmly but not overly so — hardly the type to play games or hold anyone up or looking as if he's vulgarly running for city council office. We shake hands.

Only the eighth SG in the history of the United Nations since its founding in 1945, and only the second ever to come from Asia, Ki-moon settles himself into the chair by the black piano. He takes a short breath, points to the chair opposite and looks me in the eye as if to say: Well ... I guess this is it, let's go!

It's about to be the start of our conversations.

Consider the subject matter: There's no other job like secretary general of the United Nations. It practically defines the word unique. The position offers the incumbent global star status but at the same time comes with an often-hostile bureaucracy, almost 200 bosses (UN member states), a Western media attached like crack junkies to the microwave of instant results, and a backlog of problems almost as long and snarled as history itself, including serial international gang wars deeply embedded in national DNAs.

It's a position in which the unexpected is expected as a normal daily occurrence. Does one day go by without something new and big and invariably ugly popping up somewhere on the globe and being presented as yet another UN failure?

Men who have taken on this impossible job (and all eight have been men) learn rapidly that our troubled world is orderly, well-behaved and civilised mainly in our imaginations. They find out on their first day that the magic wand for conflict resolution they thought had been left in the UN tool closet as a rightful inheritance is somehow not there. Utopia the world is not and utopia it is not going to be, anytime soon.

And so what are you — Mr. UN Big Shot — doing about this latest mess? Aren't you the almighty secretary general of the United Nations? That's why we pay you the big bucks! So what have you done for world peace lately??!!

My charged-and-ready-to-roll digital mini-video cameras are arrayed in a triangle around the chair near the piano. They are to record everything.

Ban has a little cough, nothing serious, but noticeable. He seems a little tense. Maybe a little tired.

"I gave three speeches today," he says, with a rasp.

That seems like one or two too many.

"There are days when there have been ten."

He has six speechwriters on staff. Imagine.

Ban looks at the trio of cameras and then fixes a look on me: "You should know that I have made many reports, official reports here and there on certain subjects, but I have never had any book written on me … about me … or by me."

This avoidance was due partly to his low-key style. He is certainly not a natural showboater. Part of it is due to wariness with the news media, which he may not understand — or perhaps understands all too well and wisely wants to run the other way. But since Soon-taek gave the go-ahead to this project, the project will go ahead!

"This is rare, you know, for me to meet this way, speaking what I have in my mind."

"You and me and the book, you mean this thing, now?"

He nods lightly: "There are books about me written by somebody without any interview or consultation with me. But they've been just copying, you know, what somebody has written, and whatever they can add ... there are over 10, 15 books in the Korean language. I have never read any of these books in full but sometimes people send me this book, and that book, so I realize that there are at least 10, 15 different books. This the first attempt where I'm speaking directly with somebody."

"And who's listening to you..."

"Yes."

"Does it feel good ... I mean ... so far?"

He pauses. A few seconds tick by. But you come to like this in him — a certain honest thoughtfulness that can take a little time to settle into and reveal.

"Oh, yes, yes."

I breathe a sigh of relief mentally. The secretary general has a reputation for being about as open as the CIA on a bank holiday. God bless Mrs. Ban for giving the big thumbs up!

SECRET DIARY?

I start with a long shot: "There's no super-secret diary?"

Ban smiles, shakes his head a little, and laughs. This he did not expect!

"No secret diary! But I am keeping a personal diary ... writing in Korean, a huge volume ever since I was foreign minister."

These were the years 2002–06 — nearly four years, which by

South Korean domestic politics standards is a long-distance run for a foreign minister; usually they get quickly shredded by Korea's primal politics — a year or so and out.

"Do you do the diary at night just before you go to bed, or is it in a bottom drawer of the office desk?"

He laughs, shaking his head again: "It is very difficult to keep that diary every day, so these days I put it on the tape recorder. Then I give it to my secretary — my Korean secretary — so it is only between myself and Isabel. Not even Yeo-cheol or Wan-soo know."

Those two are his close aides, who worked the full marathon run of his first term in office, and were given rewarding new assignments at the start of the second.

"And my wife may know or may not," says Ban, adding that it wouldn't make any difference because "she never interferes."

Mrs. Ban wouldn't know about a diary? *Interesting…*

He speaks in a steady medium-decibel voice, and in physical appearance he comes across as a simple man trying not to stand out, in order to fit in. He is 66 years of age and any excess of risky flair is kept out of sight … as if it might take on a life of its own, rocketing Ban out the window like Peter Pan.

"I just came back, like five minutes ago," he says, reading my mind, "from another meeting."

If the pay weren't good (well over $200,000, with many benefits) and the job not so noble and history's prestige beyond calculation, you could almost feel for him.

"Security Council?"

This is my best guess, as it might be anyone's. Security Council meetings tend to drag on, sometimes, it seems, for longer than the crisis or issue for which they were initially convened.

But Ban will only joke so much about this: A UNSG's attitude — pushy or subservient, respectful or resentful — toward the Security Council helps shape who he is at the world organization and how he plans to work. An adversarial relationship might grab the headlines but be internally self-destructive. To be able to bring issues to the attention of the Security Council is one of the few enumerated powers of the SG in the UN Charter, which actually defines the job rather vaguely.

By contrast, the Security Council itself is well defined but has evolved into an odd kind of fossil — though with teeth. Among its five permanent members with their notorious 'veto' power are the globe's Big Two: China and the United States. France, Great Britain and Russia are hanging around, too, of course, trying to hold their own against the reality of recent historical tides (which go by the name of Brazil, India, Germany, Japan, etc.). Taken together, the Big Five comprise Ban Ki-moon's immediate supervisors — those five, plus the 193 members of the UN General Assembly.

Easy management structure, right? They don't report to him, it's the other way round.

Ban shakes his head: "Oh — [sighs] — no, it's been other stuff — I've been very busy today." He wants to get this conversation thing going but he wants a breather too.

This is the storied, rancid New York August and his paper-thin raincoat is parked in the downstairs closet. He is still wearing his suit jacket, dress shirt and conservative blue tie. Have I ever seen him out of a business suit or at least not wearing a sports jacket? Trim as he is, it's certainly hard to imagine him in a gym working out (he doesn't), much less languid by a hotel swimming pool backed by serial shots of soju (never happened).

He sighs: "Very busy. Today it's not only the Security Council. I chair all these regional meetings. The League of Arab States, African Union, European Union, Organization of Islamic Cooperation ... a special one on Libya." He recites them like a weathered precinct captain reading out the Order of the Day.

He sighs again and stares out at the large wide span of window that overlooks the East River, a living flowing advertisement for pollution control. But in the bright reception room not a speck of dust has been permitted entry. All is clean and orderly.

"The last meeting went two hours. I thought it would end after one and half hours but you know how it is ... So in the middle of my meeting, I asked Yeo-cheol to communicate that you have to wait here."

Yoon Yeo-cheol, his detail-master/appointment-keeper/palace-guard, is a key member of the SG's staff. Like Ban himself, and the staff in the immediate top tier, he came to New York in 2006 from the South Korean foreign ministry, over which, some say, Ban had imposed his will and had reformed it, if you believe long-settled bureaucracies can ever be reformed.

Ban waits patiently in the chair, palms on knees, as if ready for the next bad turn in his life. We are roughly halfway through his first term, with rumors of uncertainty about a second. And this is eating at him.

In tandem with Beijing, he was the prior Bush administration's choice, not Obama's. He is unpopular with much of the UN Secretariat bureaucracy (but maybe this means he is doing his job). A Swedish official has written a widely distributed memo relentlessly uncharitable in her assessment of his leadership. So has a Norwegian diplomat. And the Western media, when it has taken note of him at all, has been unkind. He's no George Clooney, they more or less report.

Oh — is that right?

Western journalists would have to admit that ours is not a medium that cherishes the low-key. Ban's way can be, on the surface at least, so quiet as to be inaudible, the half dozen speechwriters notwithstanding, and perhaps so spice-less as to give a whole new haze to the term unflashy.

But Ban knows who he is, politely doubts that the dazzling Clooney could handle the job anyway, and is comfortable within his quiet diplomat/businessman's-suit state of mind. So what's next in this crazy, overly ambitious life I have chosen, he seems to be saying.

PAKISTAN CONNECTION

Ban stares into space: "I've been busy until the last minute, that's why I'm a little late."

He clears his throat to explain that our dinner at a café tomorrow night will be a little rushed. The floods in Pakistan are bad, half the country seems under water, he explains.

He's spending the weekend in Pakistan.

He will fly to Pakistan tomorrow night, Friday, to show the flag in person. And maybe to curry some favor with Islamabad, whose stubborn stand has all but brought the UN Conference on Disarmament to a stupid halt (it opposes controls on nukes because of India). That's the way it works too often: One nation says no — the UN cannot move.

The staff books the travel team into the last scheduled flight tomorrow from Kennedy International Airport. The plan, if he is not assassinated or if his plane doesn't explode mid-air (as did the late UNSG Dag Hammarskjold's in 1964 over the Congo), is for Ban to be back at his desk by Monday.

A nice quiet weekend with Ban Ki-moon.

Me asking: "Why are you going to Pakistan? Did someone suggest you go, or is it just that you saw the stomach-turning footage? What are the factors that make the secretary general decide to turn down a comfortable weekend here in this nice townhouse and jump to Pakistan instead, for a long flight to the other side of the globe?"

Right — and what favor does he owe the Pakistanis? They're not on the Security Council.

"I'm telling you very honestly, this is purely my decision. I had expected that this flood crisis would end a long time ago. Fifteen percent of total Pakistani territory is flooded now and we issued a flash appeal for urgent assistance. So I need to be there to express UN solidarity with the people of Pakistan, meeting with their president or prime minister. But that is secondary for me at this time. I just want to see for myself."

He clears his patchy throat again, adding to it a warm touch of green tea from the excellent China cups put out for us by residence staff.

"This is in continuation of what I did when Cyclone Nargis hit Myanmar. I went there when nobody went there, and I went to Haiti right after Haiti was hit by earthquake this year, and I went to Chile, and I went to Sichuan after the Chinese earthquake ... the Chinese appreciated that I helped mobilize international support."

Call it parachute humanitarianism, and Ban has chosen to do more of it than his predecessors. In fact, the peripatetic Korean SG has triggered criticism within the Secretariat that he should be staying home instead, minding the store, and leaving the dramatic disaster drop-ins to lower rung officials. On the other hand, there is but one secretary general. Probably a typical Pakistani who has been rained on, flooded, droned on, laughed at (by India), etc, might sincerely appreciate the UNSG's effort. Or maybe not care?

"So you'll be in Pakistan this weekend and you'll see some horrific scenes and you'll have the UN banner put up and we all hope you'll be safe, but then you'll stay a few days — and then you'll come back, and you'll be back ... when?"

"Monday morning."

"But will you feel you'll have gotten something done, that it was worth the effort?"

Maybe the Western media have him all wrong? Maybe there's more showboat to him than meets the eye?

Me adding: "It's raining like hell and they're dripping and they're full of mud and you're going to come by and joke in Korean or something with UN staff there?"

He says plainly: "Console and sympathize with them."

"You think they appreciate that, gives them a morale boost?"

"I'm sure… Whenever and wherever, people who are affected by natural disasters, they really appreciate the United Nations."

Me trying to understand: "In this case they know it's a long flight, it's hard even to get into flooded Pakistan at all right now, and you get there and the conditions are miserable. And this is to leave aside the safety issue, because some goon Al Qaeda guy might take a shot at you, or lob a bomb at your car, whatever… "

Ban calculates the impending weekend as more than 40 hours in the air and maybe 10 hours or so on Pakistani ground.

"Is someone over there now coordinating, getting you from the airport to Pakistan point A in a helicopter or something?"

Ban laughs: "I have to organize *now*. But the Pakistani government has been informed and it will coordinate."

He is to fly by commercial jet to Dubai, UAE, where he will be picked up by the Pakistani military and flown to a base.

So tomorrow's UNSG schedule, which includes another

conversation session for the book at 5pm and the above-mentioned dinner, is already filled up even beyond the 24-hour period.

Ban saying: "Then I have a telephone talk with the Sri Lankan president at 10:30 before my flight departure at 11pm. This is very important again on account of this accountability investigation of violation of human rights there."

The civil war in Sri Lanka, which lasted decades, killed many, especially minority Tamils. Some months earlier, Ban had ventured forth to Colombo on a 'quiet-diplomacy' visit, and had been rather un-quietly rebuffed.

Worldwide, Tamils thought this a humiliation, an unforgivable blunder of sheer ineptitude by the UNSG. Ban was criticized for frittering away the prestige of his office. When the 'secular pope' visits, the idea is that the faithful need to show at least gratitude, if not reverence — certainly not rank indifference. So the deal sometimes has to be pretty much put together before the UNSG goes and shows his face.

But this was to be a common complaint about his low-profile approach to high-level diplomacy. The time-honored nontransparent Asian style, which was also the patented working style of the only other Asian UNSG, U Thant from Burma (1961–71), is not everyone's cup of tea. It is certainly not the Western media's.

It isn't even that popular with some of his staff.

Once, in a remarkably candid private session, one of the UN's most hardworking high-end officials politely raised with Ban why he'd always bow, deeply, at public sessions. Wasn't he, after all, nothing less than the UN secretary general, the globe's top diplomat?

Ban stared, as if right through the brave fellow, implying: But don't you know I am Ban Ki-moon, humblest of all humble international civil servants?

The mildly admonished aide never raised the point again.

Of course, Ban is constantly self-evaluating, perhaps to excess. He knows that his first trip to Colombo was a low. They promised him everything and delivered nothing. But instead of giving up, Ban doubled down. He won't let the Sri Lankan portfolio go away. Tenacity: "That which doesn't kill you makes you stronger," goes the saying taught to every Korean schoolchild.

"I sent [Sri Lanka's president] a strong message yesterday. Now he's responding … he wants to speak to me. So tomorrow night we finish dinner as quickly as possible."

But in fact, to listen solely to the brutally critical worldwide Tamil diaspora, the hard-nosed Sri Lankan government has been little moved by the humanitarian appeals of our putative secular pope.

"Forty-five minutes at the restaurant and then let me have some time to pack and to organize my briefcase."

We book a table at Chin Chin on East 49th near Third Avenue. I know the owner, Jimmy, whose vivacious daughter Victoria had been a teaching assistant of mine at UCLA. Ban likes Jimmy's lively joint, too.

"Right, put your toothbrush and toothpaste in … So you're

going to Pakistan … I don't know how you do it, I couldn't."

He offers a shoulder shrug. "As secretary general, I have to be there to share these difficulties with Pakistan and its people. I'm working for all humanity and that's what I'm doing. People may regard this is as something which happened within Pakistan, but this has implications for millennium development goals and peace and development issues."

These goals, the attaining of which would nudge this troubled earth-planet closer to utopia, are the portfolio of UN official Robert Orr, a savvy American whose political as well as policy judgment Ban greatly depends on.

One thing is certain: Ban-man is not lazy.

"But the punishment on your body … I'm glad I'm not your personal physician. Did you know Obuchi when he was prime minister of Japan?" Obuchi died in office after a stroke in 2000. "Obuchi was like you, a hyperactive workaholic and always working the telephone … Obuchi-phone, you know?"

"Right, Obuchi-phone!"

"His doctors agreed he basically collapsed and died of overwork… "

Obuchi was aged 73 at his death, President Roh Moo-hyun was 67, Benazir Bhutto was 39 when that unusual lady was assassinated. They may not always die young in Asia but they do seem to die in special ways. I'll bet Mrs. Ban worries about the toll on her husband. We can ask her later.

NO CALL WAITING

Sudden rings from the telephone on the stand near the wall to the right of the piano. It's an old-fashioned table phone, and it seems just right for the mature aura of the second-floor study.

On various tables, VIP picture after picture is propped up. In the corner behind me is a virtual shrine to President John F. Kennedy, including a properly framed photograph of a 'good luck' note from JFK, presented by then Senator Edward Kennedy on the occasion of Ban's inaugural. The picture memorializes a White House meeting in 1961 between JFK and some visiting Korean students, of whom Ban, then 18, was one.

To the intrusion Ban apologizes with a nod, then jumps up to get it. It's fun to listen in, especially since I shouldn't.

He is irritated with the caller, a prominent international diplomat at the UN, not for the call but for committing what he regards as a diplomatic snub. Without going into undiplomatic particulars, the snub was to his wife, who was not invited to the New York wedding of the VIP diplomat's daughter.

You could tell that Ban, really hurt for his wife, is furious because he is trying so hard not to be obvious about it. At one point he even sort of giggles as if to try to lighten his touch and lower his temperature. The conversation goes no more than five minutes and ends with Ban changing the subject by informing the ambassador about the weekend.

Ban, having made his point while managing to keep his notorious temper under control, returns to the red/pink paisley 'conversation' chair and uses the five- or six-minute interruption to explain his policy of never letting phone calls pile up.

"For example, somebody telephones me, I do not make somebody wait, even while having breakfast or lunch. I just try to take the call because I believe that once you miss that opportunity … well, it may be just a few hours later or even 24 or even 48 hours later but because of time differences … other leaders are moving around too and I'm moving and so when *you* finally find the time, it may be very difficult to get to complete that call with the world leader. So that's why I always make myself available. I always try to take the call, the moment it comes in."

"In the middle of the night?"

"Sure … because of the time difference with Africa or Europe, what is it? Six or eight hours … yes, it is sometimes midnight. I am used to having to make a telephone call at 2 or 4 or 5am."

"You take these calls in your bedroom? Oh, Mrs. Ban must love that!"

"In my study." This is on the third floor, one floor up. He lets almost no one in there except Mrs. Ban.

"But by 4am you're in bed?"

"But I can go to my study. We [UN switchboard] are open 24 hours every day!"

It is one floor above but no one is supposed to see it. On its desk are top-secret documents and important files. Before the book is done, I just have to see it.

He explains why he never tries to put off a phone call: "I have noticed that everybody has a different way of managing their time. Leaders, whether they are presidents, prime ministers, foreign ministers, they are supposed to be so very busy. But however busy one may be, if you are really committed, you can find time for people."

I try this — to get Ban into the personal: "Germany's Chancellor Merkel is on the phone at 2am and she wants to talk to you. So what does your wife say? She is a heavy sleeper, I hope."

Ban laughs at that: "I have seen many others who just reserve their phone time, completely blocking calls during their down time … I'm open all 24 hours! When somebody wants to talk to me, I regard it as if somebody has knocked at my door, as if you are sitting inside your room, you have to answer, you have to open your door … you cannot just sit there."

I lob this: "But supposing you open the door and they have a gun and they want to shoot you?"

Ban hesitates and then laughs: "I have good security."

SANITY QUESTIONS

"Why are you always so diplomatic?"

I was thinking of the call I just overheard. If the ambassador did not sense Ban's personal pain and husband-y anger over the snub to his wife, the Security Council member should have been recalled home for being dumb and dumber.

"In private I'll always try to be very candid, straightforward, very honest."

"But surely this job is driving you crazy? You remember that in a column I once questioned your sanity, in that no sane person could possibly want a crazy job like this."

Ban laughs. So do I. The column ran in *The Seattle Times* and the *The Korea Times* and a few other newspapers in August 2006. It was widely picked up in Asia,

> ... I'm open all 24 hours! When somebody wants to talk to me, I regard it as if somebody has knocked at my door ... you have to open your door ... you cannot just sit there.

and of course widely noted in South Korea, where *The Korea Times* ran it, as it often does my work. My article endorsed Ban as the best qualified of the announced candidates for the job. I guess its timing was just right. The next month a Security Council vote pushed his candidacy to the General Assembly for its formal ok. The rest is history.

And so I thought to ask: "Are you insane still? Or were you always insane? How do you look at your sanity?"

I was only half-joking. Not everyone of sound mind would or could want this job. Early on, a well-known Singaporean official had an open shot at it but didn't like the then current unofficial job description. *Wanted: a UNSG who would be more secretary than general.*

Ban shifts his weight in the chair and stares at me for a few seconds with a wan smile: "Many people have been asking me [clearing throat] if I am enjoying my job. My answer is that this is not about whether I enjoy it or not. This is a job that requires a sense of mission. Many people had cautioned me that this was going to be the most impossible job. I realize now, after having served, that this really is the most impossible job. And jokingly I told my member states and my friends that my mission would be to make this impossible job a mission possible ... mission *possible*. That's what I'm doing — whether I'm sane or insane."

> This is a job that requires a sense of mission ... I realize now, after having served, that this really is the most impossible job.

We've all have had jobs that threatened to drive us crazy, right?

Ban nodding: "Unless you have a very strong sense of commitment to public service, it will be extremely difficult. One night I felt I had given up. But then, for me, during all my 40-plus years as a diplomat, I had been living with a strong sense of public service, and so sometimes, in a sense, my personal life, by the standard of some Westerners, might have been considered miserable. Somebody said in a sarcastic way that I have been working like a slave."

Did Ban misinterpret what might have been meant as sympathy? During the first two or three years of his first term, flat-out compliments and positive endorsements were hard for him to come by. After a while the man might not have recognized a compliment when it came his way.

"But that kind of somewhat humiliating comment didn't bother me. I have always put public service first, then second comes my personal or private life, because [to do this job properly] I have to almost neglect my personal family life here. I'm deeply grateful to my wife who has never complained."

Given his punishing, even masochistic schedule, someone might wish to declare her a living saint. In effect, she can be thought of as a public servant as well. (They celebrated their 40th wedding anniversary in 2011.)

> I have always put public service first, then second comes my personal or private life, because [to do this job properly] I have to almost neglect my personal family life here.

"I'm extremely lucky to have such a woman, devoted totally to family and even public service. There is no regret for me about our relationship. I think that I have been doing what I should do. That's not only during my time as secretary general but even during my previous capacities as foreign minister and many other small or medium positions of importance — my life is just devoted to public service."

In fact, that has been his entire life. No detours into the richness of the private sector. No cushy university appointments to catch his breath for the next plunge back into the cold waters of international diplomacy. No throwaway weekends playing golf with the buddies. The straight and steady Ban says to himself: *Keep going as you have been going and don't look back.*

This is probably the longest span of time Ban has ever set aside for a conversation with an outsider. Yet he is not impatient, and seems almost close to comfortable. The posture is not of a man on the rack but rather of a man thinking the worst is behind him and life will get better.

ECONOMY TRAVEL

Me saying: "To date, you've taken a pounding from the media, particularly the British and Western press; and you have this long-dug-in bureaucracy here, and scores of recalcitrant member states, and so you have all kinds of issues with the five permanent members of the Security Council ... but you look pretty good! What's your secret? You eat a lot of kimchi?"

He does laugh at that: "People wonder what kind of exercise I do. I normally don't do exercise — even in the morning hours I'm too busy to spend the time. And basically I have not been enjoying exercise. I have just been sleeping well."

"Like when you hit the pillow do you just drop?"

"Yes, I just sleep but I do not sleep long. Maximum five hours, but sometimes I have to sleep for just a few hours, particularly when I travel; and then you have to endure 36 hours or 40 hours without being able to sleep. But that I am accustomed to, though sometimes it is extraordinarily difficult, with very tough schedules."

Do people who sleep longer, live longer? Being sleep-deprived while staying human is a quality not all of us have. "Some people can do it but that kind of travel gets to a lot of people."

His response is a shrug: "The difference between me and a secretary of state, or the American president, is that they have their own plane but I do not. I have to travel mostly on commercial airlines, and sometimes I travel economy, when there are no other seats."

This seems astonishing: "The people running the airline won't kick somebody out for you? The UN doesn't provide a dedicated plane for its secretary general?"

He shakes his head: "Sometimes it is quite embarrassing. I travel with my own staff. I mean sometimes when there are absolutely no seats, there is no choice, then you have to sit in economy."

Surprising, no? "Out there, people assume that the secretary general enjoys a kind of life on this golden throne, where people feed you stuffed grape leaves and all but clean and dress you."

"Oh no no no no no no."

Even visitors, especially from South Korea, to the otherwise excellent townhouse residence are surprised that Donald Trump grandiose it really is not. People knowledgeable about Manhattan real-estate values would rightly size it up to cost millions. But the Taj Mahal … no.

Ban continuing: "Well, there is one important thing about the airplane. Sometimes you have to wait hours at an airport to change planes for a transfer — that's a waste for any secretary general of the UN. Because of that, many member states have suggested some special aircraft for the secretary general but…"

"They know what the media will do with that story!"

His face almost blanches white: "Media?!! They will be very negative."

"You wouldn't need a 737, you could probably do with an executive jet. How many staffers do you travel with, ordinarily?"

"Normally 20, including security."

"You could have an executive jet, like a Gulfstream or something. You could lease it."

"We were considering leasing but somehow even that presents image problems."

"Can't rich member states help out?"

"My predecessors enjoyed some hospitality from some rich member states and in fact I do enjoy such hospitality from rich member states, who, very generously, provide a plane sometimes. That has been quite effective. I can plan according to my time, I can leave at any time late at night or early in the morning. But when you have to depend on commercial airlines then the whole of your schedule is dependent upon commercial schedules. That makes your mobility very difficult."

"So there are two categories of travel for you. One is the trip that is planned in advance where you can get a member state to help. But then with emergency travel, you have to scramble and get whatever's available."

He nods: "I wanted to visit Chile after the disastrous earthquake [in February 2010]. As the secretary general, of course, I really wanted to be there. But so did all the Chilean people living in the US who rightly wanted to visit their families."

"And so did all the celebrities who wanted to go there and do their thing."

He smirks — right! "There were absolutely no airplane seats available going to Chile. I had to give up finally. But then the President-elect at that time, now current President Pinera, managed to help. He had to cancel eight seats which were already booked and we were able to visit Chile and that was a big help. But on several occasions I was almost on the verge of cancelling a trip because of the unavailability of seats."

Given all that people and the media seem to ask of a secretary general, does making him into a 'diplomat without wings' make any sense?

Me pursuing: "Say you get on a plane for a 15-hour flight to Cairo, and you get out and you go to the hotel. Now, because you have to meet the President of Egypt or whatever, do you get an hour to get yourself together, for a shower and a change of clothes, then you meet with your staff, or do you sometimes go right from the airport to the meeting?"

"Many cases where I had to directly go to meeting places or even if I had to go to the hotel, I was given 15 minutes to a half hour. That was sometimes inhuman treatment!" He laughs. "I don't have time even to shave! So in such a case what do you do? When that situation is foreseen, I do my shaving on the airplane to make myself presentable!"

Me saying: "Because you know you're going to get the cameras in your face the minute you get off the flight…"

"One of my predecessors advised me this way when I was elected secretary general: 'When you travel, you should plan one day ahead of the official schedule. Take one full day to rest, otherwise it will be very difficult.' But I never accepted his advice. I have always been arriving very early in the morning in European countries or Africa, and starting immediately. Then you have to endure almost 36 hours or 40 hours before you can sleep."

"Can you sleep on an airplane?"

He nods yes.

"Do you take a sleeping pill or something?"

"No sleeping pill."

"And you really don't drink, right, a little wine or something?"

"I take one or two glasses of wine, but I cannot sleep for more than two hours or so because of the preparation needed for the next meeting. Sometimes I have to read all this material on the airplane and that's the only time available."

"You're the one who has to be an expert on everything?"

"My accompanying staff may just sleep, watch a movie. I don't have any time. I have to read."

"Maybe by the second term you'll have everything memorized?"

"When you are going to meet somebody then you have to be prepared specifically. If I'm out until 10pm or so, and I don't have time to come back to my hotel, then I have to take all the materials … all the talking points in my pockets."

"You don't leave them with an aide?"

"Maybe a big upsized speech text I'd ask my aides to carry. But I have to be ready. You don't know what situation you will be exposed to, so I carry them. It's better for me, it's better for the insurance of my mind, peace of my mind."

"Peace of mind."

"Just to keep everything in my pocket, including the back pocket."

"Ban Ki-moon's 'cheat' sheets..."

"I say jokingly, I'm carrying all my ammunition-bullets in my pockets, so I need to use all these bullet points and firepower whenever required. As SG I have to learn many issues beyond that which I dealt with when I was foreign minister, starting from political and peace issues and human rights and development issues, like disease and health issues and education and food and fuel, climate change."

"Does your head ever explode?"

"I try to maintain it all in my head."

Happiness is probably relative. Workaholics work on holidays without becoming self-critical. It's just the way they are and what they do. Their worst days are usually when they have the day off. What will they ever do with all that time?

> As SG I have to learn many issues beyond that which I dealt with when I was foreign minister, starting from political and peace issues and human rights and development issues, like disease and health issues and education and food and fuel, climate change.

UN FIRST LADY

The trim Ban seems always on the go, and it is the next day, early Friday evening, when it would be normal to begin winding down for the week. Ban, instead, is fully expecting his third wind (is there a Korean gene informally called Red Bull?) and thinking about how little Urdu he knows.

Yoo Soon-taek[1] comes into the study. She is a Korean woman of middle height and stolid build, with a carriage of extraordinary ethereal calm. Her hair is bunched back tidily and her floor-length dress is a lightly decorated color-neutral cotton shift that looks well chosen to ward off the assault of Manhattan humidity even in the summer. Her eyes seem to take in everything quickly, without any suggestion of bossiness.

"Dinner, anyone?" asks Mrs. Ban.

She has agreed to join us at Chin Chin. She sits down in a chair not remotely in the line of the crossfire of our conversation.

I look at Ban: "I don't mean to be crude or vulgar, but just whatever you're comfortable with. Share a bit about your relationship with this woman that you've been with your adult life. I mean you come home and you've been beaten up by the press or somebody on the staff has screwed up or maybe you've messed up — does she help you or does she ignore you, does she not desire to know about the office, or is she actively interested in it? How does that work?"

---

1 Normal Korean usage prefers leaving even the married woman with the patronymic. And, in usual East Asian style, father's name goes first. Hereinafter, I will use either Mrs. Ban or, informally, Soon-taek.

Mrs. Ban settles quietly on the couch to my right. I first met her at Ban's installation as Kofi Anan's successor in December 2006. My wife and I had been put in the guest box to the far right of the central podium of the cavernous General Assembly. In front of us was the striking Nane and her husband Kofi Annan, who, when he walked in to sit next to Nane, prompted my wife Andrea (who had never seen him in person) to exclaim: "Oh my gosh … the lion king."

The glamour gap between the Annans and the Bans was irrelevant to my wife, who could not have cared less about it. Raised in Hollywood, she has no respect for the media's narcotic dependency on superficial charisma. But she also knew right at that moment, just before his installation, that the Charisma Gap will prove a problem for the Bans — a brutal fact of modern mass-media life.

Ban saying: "I would rather characterize my wife as a person who really possesses and practices the ideal virtue of a woman. Particularly in Asian culture, the virtue of her place in the family; at least in my generation, the wife is first of all very faithful to family. Soon-taek is, as we say, a wise woman and a good wife and mother, and the level of tolerance on her part is very deep and high." He almost sighs when he says this.

He *should* sigh. Even now he can't offer quality time over the weekend, just like back in 2005 when I visited him in Seoul! (See "The Korean Connection" on page 57.)

"As in tolerance for you and your insane lifestyle?"

"Yeah, that's right."

Mrs. Ban smiles a little. It is hard to imagine this former Korean librarian ever raising her voice.

Me saying: "Because you're never around!"

She smiles again.

Ban stays in control, without overtly asserting it: "It's her tolerance for understanding others' positions, and she rarely expresses her emotions, she always tries to be patient before she speaks out for her own position. So she always tries to respect my work and we normally don't discuss things that happen in the office … almost none, except if there was some interesting gossip!"

"Fun gossip?"

"Yes, fun gossip."

"Not serious geopolitical gossip?"

Soon-taek smiles demurely.

Me suggesting: "Like so and so is getting divorced or so and so ambassador from a very important Asian country got drunk or something like that."

Ban averts my eyes and avoids specifics: "We normally try to talk, but because of my very hectic schedule, sometimes it's very difficult to find time with my wife, even on weekends. Sometimes when I have free time, even on weekends, I have to prepare for the following weeks' schedules. I'm just overpowered by so many things to read and so many things to do and so many telephone calls to make. My wife fully understands and that has allowed me during the last 40 years as a public servant to be able to devote my

time fully and wholly to carrying out my 'official duty'."

They have three offspring: "You are almost saying you were an absentee father, always traveling or working in the office."

He chuckles: "That's right. And without her support, patience and understanding I might not have been able to be here in fact."

I have to laugh: "Well, if it were America, you'd probably be divorced! Do you think she knew early on that she was marrying a crazy person like you?"

That one makes him pause: "I'm sure that she is happy with me [laughs]."

Mrs. Ban smiles.

"Have you told her yet that you're going to Pakistan?"

Ban coughs uncomfortably.

Soon-taek says nothing and shows no emotion.

"Er, no … I have to … tell her now. I just came back from my office."

"So you told your inner staff first, the president of the Security Council second, me third and your wife fourth. Now, is she going to hit you over the head with a broomstick and say, can't you stay home for once?"

Ban trills out in laughter. "I don't know … she will support me."

"She will support you?"

"All the time she supports me. I leave everything as far as household affairs are concerned to her."

"She probably even balances your checkbook and stuff. Because if you did it, you'd be three months behind in paying your bills, right?"

Soon-taek smiles broadly.

He nods: "She also has been very active in the diplomatic community. She's been participating in diplomatic wives' associations all the time. She's been meeting regularly with Security Council spouses. And when I do travel with her, there's always some program for my wife, visiting nurseries and education facilities or hospitals, and trying to care for all those vulnerable people."

"Not to be glib, but the Lady Di role of being the First Lady of the UN — does she like it?"

Soon-taek nods almost imperceptibly.

Her husband: "Oh yes. She really volunteers and she's also busy in terms of public activities."

Me saying: "So in a way, long ago, she said, this is my life, this is my fate [both Bans laugh] and so it gives you a measure of comfort to know that if she was going to complain or object she would've done it long ago ...[corner phone rings] You better really get the phone ... it's probably the president of Pakistan!"

Ban gets the phone: "Yes? Hello? Ambassador DiCarlo, how are you? Yes, yes, I just wanted to mention that I'm going to visit Pakistan, on a humanitarian mission, of course. I cannot just sit here, we really should make an appearance there. As secretary general I think I need to show concern for all these disasters — Myanmar, Chile, Haiti and China. I think it's time for me to visit Pakistan and express my solidarity to these people and discuss what the UN and international aid groups can do. I'm just letting you know for your information. I hope you can pass this on to Ambassador Susan Rice and Secretary Clinton. I think I'm going there by commercial airplane and will meet the prime minister, then I'll come back on Monday morning ... yes, there is security. But I'm just making it very confidential ... our people have many security people on the ground. Ok, all right. I see, I see, thank you very much, Ambassador DiCarlo. Bye-bye."

Ban turns back to us: "Ok, no more disruptions now!"

He was talking to Ambassador Rosemary A. DiCarlo, U.S. Deputy Permanent Representative to the United Nations. Ban explains that we are in Manhattan and this is August and a lot of officials are out of town: "U.S. ambassador Susan Rice is on vacation, and I had informed the Russian ambassador, who right now is president of the Security Council, so he should know and the American ambassador should know [my Pakistan travel plan]. But this is very strictly limited to maybe 10 people who know."

"Did Yeo-cheol get the supersaver fare for you?"

Ban laughs and nods like, yeah, right. He sits down but the phone rings again. He lets out what seems like a silent sigh, returns to the phone table, picks it up, mumbles a few indistinct words, and then says something and puts it down, promising we won't be disturbed any more.

It looks like his vow not to keep callers waiting is being put to a severe test.

Returning to his wife: "She's a great, soft person, and she's not one for speaking much, but sometimes when she speaks…"

"Well, you know, there's an expression in America called 'pillow power'. Have you ever heard of that?"

"Pillow power? Yes."

"Does she have pillow power?"

"Uh… [laughs] I respect her, and have been with her for 40 years."

CONVERSATIONS WITH MRS. BAN,
MAY 2012

Mrs. Ban sometimes took part in our conversations but rarely stepped out of the shadow of her husband (a phenomenon she mentions below). So I put some questions to her that she said she might answer in e-mail fashion. She did.

When you and your husband came into this important situation, you told us you got some good advice from Mrs. Kofi Annan. Now that you and your husband are more than halfway through his 10-year run as UNSG, what advice would you give to the spouse of the next SG? Mrs. Waldheim [the wife of former UN SG Kurt Waldheim] advised me that I would need to get used to the feeling of isolation and exclusion when you are standing next to your husband while he is getting all the spotlight and cheers from everybody around. After having spent five years with him, I now totally agree with what she told me. After getting pushed by all those fans welcoming the secretary general, I always get behind and wonder awkwardly where I should be.

Mrs. Annan told me to look for anything that I want to do for myself. Now I understand that what she meant was to find ways to utilize my own time, not to be a burden on your husband who is so busy around the clock. Mrs. Annan had talent for painting, which kept her happy and busy on her own.

In the UN community, spouses of representatives of 193 member states organize cultural events, fund-raisers, lunches and other social gatherings to promote their own countries and their causes. I try as much as possible to attend those events hosted by spouses and to get to know them. Sometimes my schedules are too crowded and tight, but once I am there, I learn a lot from them and build a sense of solidarity with them. New York, and the United Nations for that matter, is a unique place where you can meet the most diverse people from around the world. In that sense, I would advise the spouse of my husband's successor that meeting nice people and building friendships with them is such a pleasure which will enrich and deepen your life more than ever.

It seems there is no fixed definition of the role of the spouse of the secretary general. I made it a rule to have my own visits to various UN projects in my own program whenever I accompany my husband on his trips. As I listened to the women and children in those countries and the UN staff and NGOs who help them under very difficult circumstances, I came to understand better what my husband is working so hard for and what the UN is about. I try to come to them with my humble hope that my little gestures could be some source of encouragement for them. For the spouse of the next SG, I would also advise her or him to find one's own area of interest which will also help define the role as spouse of the secretary general, and such work will be remembered as one's own accomplishment and it will give her or him a lot of rewarding feelings.

It goes without saying that our own health is the most important, before anything else. She (if the next SG is again male and has a female partner, that is) may need regular exercise to keep her up. New York is such a dynamic city where she can explore a wide variety of cultures.

Do you use or want an 'advisor' on fashion? How do you know what to wear to these VIP events where you are so prominent?

Well, the UN SG and his spouse are often invited to VIP events but they are not the kind of events where you find too much glamour and vanity, as they are usually events about those causes the United Nations is dedicated to, like fighting poverty, AIDS or enhancing children and maternal health. I don't think the variety of my wardrobe will be enough to hire an advisor on fashion. Whenever there are high profile occasions, I think about the meaning of the events and try to choose the most appropriate dresses that can present the secretary general and me as just another ordinary but sincere couple.

Are there aspects to being the SG's wife that are NOT negative? Or is the atmosphere so rarified and difficult that it is impossible to relax and enjoy?

Of course, I am a shy person who is still not used to the spotlight we are getting and I am constantly worried about my husband's mental and physical health when he works so hard and travels so much.

However, there are many positive sides to being the wife of the secretary general that I feel happy about. When I witness my husband's work and join him on his trips to the field, I can learn a lot, see a larger world, and better notice cultural and historical differences between countries. But what is more important is that now I can see how we can help those people who need us. When we can witness their plight and offer our hand and solidarity, I get such an uplifting sense of gratitude to be able to help them. Isn't that the biggest reward?

You seem to have a special sensibility about, and love for, movies. Are we right about that? Any special favorites? What kinds of movies do you like most?

I do enjoy watching movies. Like literature, movies allow us to have wider experiences about who we are and about human nature in general through those characters in movies.

I like those movies that give you a closer look at the meaning of life by means of drama and help you to get a better understanding about the human condition. In that regard, I like dramas which deal with humanity or specific characters, while my husband prefers action movies. So we have a little quarrel whenever we have to choose between the two different genres. Mostly, I let him have fun and join him. I go to the movies I prefer with my friends.

There are many movies that I like but I have seen *Gone with the Wind* many times. I liked *The Queen*, *Julie and Julia* and *The Iron Lady*, which touched me with the human sides of the main characters by the excellent performances of Helen Mirren and Meryl Streep. Among the recent ones, I really enjoyed *The Artist*.

There is a movie titled *Yesterday*, a South African movie from 2004 that was directed by Darell Roodt and starred Leleti Khumalo. This is a movie that tells you about the stigma and discrimination against HIV/AIDS patients. At the same time, it shows the power of love and a woman's strength through a mother who was AIDS-infected. I saw that movie three times and cried a lot. When I empathize with the characters of a movie and shed my own tears for them, I find myself purified after such cathartic moments.

Women in Seoul, compared to women in New York — how different are they today?

Socio-economic changes in Korea have taken place very rapidly. So did the definition of the average Korean woman, particularly in Seoul. Now, women in Seoul are as smart, sophisticated and independent as those in New York. I heard that the TV show *Sex and the City* is so popular in Korea and many Korean young ladies travel to New York and visit the neighborhood of the heroines of the drama. On the other hand, I am a little concerned about the materialistic and demonstrative tendency among women in Seoul, exemplified by their obsession about luxury goods and sporting the most up-to-date fashion.

What progress have women made in South Korea? How have their prospects and hopes changed?
The life of women of my mother's generation was characterized by their sufferings from colonialism, the Korean war, the social constraints coming from a traditional feudal way of life and lack of access to education, which led to illiteracy for most of them.

My generation had the benefit of access to higher education but we were educated to become 'a wise mother and good wife'. During those days, we still had prevalent discrimination, with the unspoken rule that women should resign from workplaces once they got married.

These days, Korean women are enjoying good education without much discrimination. I don't think there are any more companies who reject them just for being women. They would all want to build their careers at nice workplaces of their choice and would wish to have the moment of their own achievements.

Now, they say that for Korean women, marriage is a choice, not a necessity. They tend to get married at a later stage and have babies much later than before or, for some, have none at all.

However much the life around us changes, the importance of family should be respected all the time. In order to maintain such an environment, we need support from our community as well as from within the family, for women's desire to be recognized and have their own roles in society.

Don't we need happy women, to have happy families, sound society and a peaceful world?

I have to say the lady revealed in the replies above is very much the Yoo Soon-taek I have met and probably seems the woman most people at the UN and in the Korean diplomatic world know: honest, direct and, somehow — for all the ups-and-downs in her husband's career, the changes of climates and cultures, and the challenges — a real, modest and, truth be told, nobody's fool kind of woman.

YOU WOULDN'T ABANDON A SHIP
IN A STORM JUST BECAUSE YOU
COULDN'T CONTROL THE WINDS.

– Utopia

The Korean Connection

The quiet Confucian … future foreign minister …
getting sacked … Powell telephones

I FIRST MET Ban Ki-moon in 2005. It was a March Saturday in Seoul and the then foreign minister had just spent the week ushering then U.S. Secretary of State Condoleezza Rice around the Korean Peninsula as if she were royalty. The massive press reviews in the Korean media were very good for him, and he was in a chipper mood. He was planning a potentially dicey trip to Tokyo very soon, and as we sat down along with two foreign ministry aides over breakfast, he turned the discussion to how best to ease Korean-Japanese relations.

The session lasted nearly two hours and, almost oddly, Ban seemed in no rush to end it. He laughed when I kiddingly speculated about the reaction of Mrs. Ban (whom I had not met till then) when informed by her husband that he would be away for breakfast on Saturday morning too. This is after being out the entire week, mainly showing Secretary Rice the sights, including the infamous northern land border with North Korea, and smoothing out bumps in U.S.-Korean relations. "Who is this Plate guy?" Mrs. Ban must have quipped, was my guess. "Is this something you *have* to do?" At that, I remember, Ban chuckled.

We were settled around a table in the Ninth Gate dining room of the Chosun Hotel. This was in the center of the sprawling capital, a madcap metropolis that looks to me as if laid out by an LSD committee. In the restaurant foyer, you see framed pictures of American icons Bob Hope and Muhammad Ali and your heart sinks and you begin to worry about the foreign minister's taste in dining out! But then an utter vision hits you and you realize this place is rather special. Through panoramic windows, your eyes hit the gorgeous Ninth Gate Garden, with the centerpiece jewel, the Temple of Heaven. It is a knockout — if a knockoff of the original from China. Guidebooks describe the Ninth Gate as one of Asia's most romantic restaurants. I turned to Ban and he saw the effect on me. Proud of Korea and being a Korean, he wanted to show off this place to the visiting American.

That week turned out to be a career-shaping one for the Korean foreign minister. A few years later Secretary Rice and her Chinese counterpart would agree at a secret get-together in a suite in New York's Waldorf Astoria Hotel on Ban as their candidate to succeed Kofi Annan. For this ambitious Korean's candidacy, that was to be like heaven and earth coming together. It was then, really, all but a done deal.

THE QUIET CONFUCIAN

Beijing was comfortable with Ban because under the somewhat leftist President Roh, the foreign policy of South Korea, ordinarily little more than a staunch U.S. ally, seemed to tilt China-ward and Ban had gone out of his way to come up with reasons to visit Beijing and its diplomats. Yet Rice had spent enough time with Ban that week to ascertain that he was anything but the second coming of a Khmer Rouge.

What's more, in his tenure as foreign minister Ban had travelled enough to establish his image as a true internationalist. In fact, the quiet Confucian Korean seemed no careering Kofi-mate in style, but more of a diligent and loyal secretary than a blustering and unpredictable general.

We reminisced about this 2005 meeting in the second-floor reception room of his residence five years later: "There used to be a joke about the South Korean foreign minister, whoever he was ... that Korean foreign policy was so terribly parochial and regional that when the foreign minister of Korea got on an airplane for foreign diplomacy, he didn't have to pack an overnight bag."

Ban laughs. He'd heard that one.

"But when you came in, observers said you sought to broaden what a South Korean foreign minister would do — and so you went all over the place. Was that because the Kennedy School deepened your international vision, or was it because Korean foreign policy was just too parochial? Or was it because in the back of your mind, you were campaigning for the job of secretary general, which you knew would go to someone from Asia; or was it all three of the above in some proportion?"

Ban shakes his head: "Not because of the UN candidacy but

because I believe that Korean foreign policy had been too focused on just four powers … the powers surrounding the Korean Peninsula."

This is what Koreans call their "difficult neighborhood". Perhaps Ban and his allies were nowhere near putting together their now-famous American style 2006 campaign to install a Korean atop the UN. But the suddenly higher profile for Korean diplomacy did complement the credibility of Ban's candidacy when it was announced the following year.

Ban explaining: "Back then, even to Europeans, we didn't talk much, and we didn't know much about Europe, let alone Africa. So I proposed to President Roh Moo-hyun that we visit Africa. Only one Korean had gone before, President Chun Doo-hwan, 26 years before. I talked to President Roh and said let's also visit Turkey. Turkey is a country aligned with the U.S. during the Korean War, and since the end of the Korean War, all Turkey's senior people had visited Korea. But nobody from our country had visited Turkey. When I was deputy foreign minister, I was the highest officer to visit Turkey. So as the foreign minister, I advised President Roh: 'You have to visit Turkey, we need to be seen as a country whose people know gratefulness. We should thank them.'"

"Because Turkey was involved on your side in the Korean War?"

"Oh yes. But then I went to Greece too. I really wanted to expand our diplomatic horizon. I visited Arab countries, where so many Koreans had construction businesses. So Korea was best known for commercial trade. But our diplomatic efforts should have been commensurate with those activities."

"Would you say that it could be argued that BKM is the first modern foreign minister of South Korea?" It's an obvious compliment of course but it is also something of a fact.

"I don't think there will be much opposition to that. And I was one of the longest serving foreign ministers. Most foreign ministers are fired after one year or 10 months or even five months. So there was not that much continuity. But during my time I was able to expand my own network, able to have my own plans, diplomatic policies."

"And President Roh gave you that space."

"Oh yes, yes."

"That's good because he had his share of domestic and political problems as you know."

"He used to call me his tutor. When I was diplomatic advisor, or as you might put it, national security advisor, he said, well Ambassador Ban, we have a foreign minister, so let him carry out his duty as foreign minister, but you serve as tutor for me, because I do not know much about foreign policy."

That's an amazing admission by a head of state. But — in his case — an honest one.

"Roh was open-minded, candid and the type of person who could not hide anything in his heart."

"When you heard that he committed suicide ... were you surprised?" In 2009 ex-President Roh, who had appointed Ban foreign minister, and championed Ban's UNSG candidacy, jumped off a cliff, killing himself. He and his relatives had been under investigation for possible corruption.

"I was so surprised. But I thought that his character, his way of thinking, might have driven him to suicide."

"Why? What do you mean?"

"He must have been very humiliated."

"By the accusations of the scandal?"

"By the accusations. He couldn't endure this kind of … losing face … humiliation."

The Korean political culture is not Scandinavian style squeaky-clean. Transparency International, the Europe-based nonprofit that assesses corruption-perception levels nation by nation, routinely puts Sweden, Norway and Denmark (and, for that matter, Singapore) at the apex of the clean-as-a-whistle top. But not South Korea, which rates a dismal #43 spot, well below the U.S. (which, at 24th on the list, is itself no prize) and Japan (which in 2011 was viewed as 14th least corrupt in the world).

Me asking: "Now that you're in a higher profile position than even the president of South Korea, aren't you scared to death that some relative will do something screwy and you'll be blamed for it and so forth, or maybe your people don't need to be told that you'll chop their heads off if they do something silly to compromise you?"

I remember a Korean diplomat colleague of Ban saying no one works harder than Ki-moon and the UN would never get "a Kofi Annan-type scandal on his watch".

Poor Kofi, who prior to the 2005 Iraqi oil-for-food scandal had been viewed as the very model of international-civil-servant rectitude. But the UN is a huge forest where much is shaded and dark canyons are everywhere. Any secretary general can wake up in the morning and be under fire for a mess in a corner of that forest he scarcely knew existed. In Annan's case, though, the mess hit close to home when his son Kojo was alleged to have pocketed millions from the program.

Ban believes nothing like this can happen on his watch: "I have been maintaining my life as a man of honesty and integrity. First of all, I was born in a very poor family and I have lived that way…"

I reply: "Sure, but many people are born in poor families and they become corrupt, perhaps precisely for that very reason."

> I have been maintaining my life as a man of honesty and integrity. First of all, I was born in a very poor family and I have lived that way…

"No. When I married, my wife was also from a very poor family without father and single mother and didn't have anything. Early on, when I was living in New York 30 years ago, I had to worry about my living conditions."

"Paying the rent?" Having once been so poor would hardly seem like a corruption incubator for corruption temptation

"Yeah, paying rent and paying my gas bill, insurance. I insured my automobile from Arizona!"

"Cheaper to do it from Arizona?"

"Much cheaper. So I know about poverty and I had been

making accountability and ethics the number one priority and virtue."

I try this: "Would you have any worries that a member of your staff or your family might be doing something behind your back that's going to blow up in your face?"

"I don't think so. It was I that established the United Nations ethics office. There was no such ethics office in the United Nations and I applied this to all UN funds and programs. It was established after the oil-for-food scandal. Member states wanted to have some stronger scrutiny over procurements and so on."

"No oil-for-food with BKM? So I can write this book and assert that three years from now you'll still be good?"

He nods gravely.

"You talked yesterday about public service. Where does this passion for public service come from? Why not just be a lawyer, work 60 hours a week and come home every night and be in your own bed 90 percent of the time?"

"First of all I have been educated to put public service, public good, first, then personal matters." Ban refers to some ancient books about public service, drawn from Chinese as well as Korean ancestry, that define exemplary conduct by the public servant.

"Basically when I was a young boy, I thought the only way for me to contribute to my country was through public service, because Korea was so poor at that time and without letting Korea become better known to other countries and without having a good relationship with America and other big powers in the world, we would have no place to stand.

"That had a strong influence on my mind and, luckily, I was able to be admitted to college, where I majored in international relations at Seoul National University, and luckily again I was able to pass the Korean civil service examination to become a diplomat. Since those very early junior days as a government official, I really tried to lead by example, practice by example.

"To lead by example has been my guiding principle. Even as secretary general, my first word to our UN staff and also to the member states is that I will lead by example. Watch me, and if I do anything outside this boundary, then they should challenge me. It is quite easy to say, but it's very difficult to practice in fact. You have to always be more exemplary than other people, in terms of work ethics; in terms of public service you have to always be in the front, ahead of everybody."

"But as you look back now over your life ... the motor, the fire, the intensity inside of you, when do you think you first might have felt that you had that? When you were eight years old or 16 years old? Or when you saw

> **To lead by example has been my guiding principle ... Watch me, and if I do anything outside this boundary, then they [UN staff] should challenge me ... You have to always be more exemplary than other people, in terms of work ethics; in terms of public service you have to always be in the front, ahead of everybody.**

the American G.I.s save Korea or when you saw poor people in the rural area? You were born in a very poor area."

"I was one of the very poor students."

"So when was the spark ignited? Is there something you can look back to and say, maybe that's why I am where I am today?"

"My father, a normal humble Korean at that time, was a company official and he was good at Chinese calligraphy. He really wanted to teach me such correct things and so I was influenced by my father. My father was more generous and flexible, but in a sense my mother was rather strict, stricter than my father. I was a very good child without making any problem. If I made any mistake, my father used to pick up the rod and hit me, as a way of education. That's what most Korean fathers and mothers did at that time. They wanted to educate their children correctly and I was educated in that atmosphere. When the Korean War broke out, I was just six years old, just one year before I went to school. Then when I went to school, after the Korean War, the school buildings had been destroyed, we had no place to study, we had only the school yard. There we would sit on the dirt, and under the shadow of the trees, and when it rained we had to run … all the students into the small auditorium which was spared from the destruction. At the time … I was in the first grade? Second grade? Maybe eight years old? Nine years old?"

"And you still remember this?"

"Of course, of course. There were no classrooms with walls, but the experience gave me good stories to inspire the children of developing countries, such as when I was visiting African countries and their primary schools. There I saw many students studying in proper classrooms. Of course these classrooms were overcrowded. In one class there were 120 students or so, but I told them to feel lucky that they have a school with classrooms and walls and blackboards and desks. When I was a young boy like them, I didn't even have classrooms, I had to study on the dirt until they were able to build proper classrooms."

I doubt that story helped the African students feel better about their situation.

"Then I was in high school, and at that time I was selected as one of just four Korean students from throughout the country as Red Cross representative and I was dispatched to the U.S. I was no more than a country boy who didn't have anything. Then coming to San Francisco, thanks to the Red Cross program — it was a total shock. Normally people say it was culture shock, but it was much, much more than that!"

We both laugh. It is hard to see him now as a country bumpkin from Korea.

"I had never been out of Seoul, and it was the first time in an airplane. It was in 1962 and I was18 years old. It was big news at that time in my small village because a young Korean high school student was dispatched to the U.S.! Then I spent one month traveling to San Francisco, and from there to Portland, Oregon, then Spokane, Washington, then I came to Washington DC. There we were assembled with other international students and invited to the White House to meet President Kennedy. It was the most inspiring and most exciting moment for any of us students."

"And you still remember that today?"

"Yes, yes. I have that text of his remarks at the White House and the picture, still."

"You have that on your desk or something?"

"Yes, yes, I have it here now in my study. It was given to me by Senator Edward Kennedy. I was very moved. What happened was, there were newspaper stories that when I was a young boy I had the extraordinary experience of meeting President Kennedy, which inspired me to become a diplomat, and which led me to become secretary general. [The late] Senator Edward Kennedy read this story and he checked with the Kennedy Presidential Library and had the photograph of us students with JFK and the remarks that were made by President Kennedy at that time copied. And then he brought me the whole thing with a nice frame. I can show it to you!"

Ban stands up and walks to a side table behind me. There it is — the framed photograph of (1) JFK's remarks, (2) a picture of the young Korean kids, including the young Ban peeking through in the back with an impish smile, and (3) a personal note from JFK's only surviving brother at that time, Edward (Teddy) Kennedy.

"That was the moment when I seriously considered my future. I was very busy studying but I made up my mind that the best way would be to become a diplomat and work for my country."

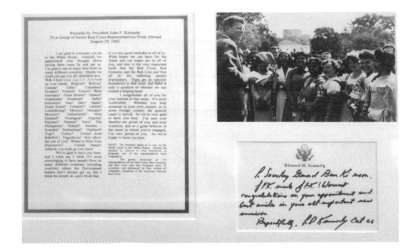

FUTURE FOREIGN MINISTER

Ban says his 10 months at Harvard between 1984 and 1985 took his foreign-policy sophistication to the next level. The educational methodology was not like anything he'd encountered in his Korea.

I put it this way: "The Korean learning style is, you receive the great wisdom of the professor!" That was the old-fashioned Asian way of university instruction.

Ban confirms: "We received and we read and we memorized, exactly according to what the teachers taught us. There was one-way-traffic teaching at Seoul National University. But at Harvard it was a kind of mutual two-way traffic and I learned a more analytical way of approaching things. Before that my belief was that knowledge itself is time bound: When time goes by, you are apt to forget all the details ... facts, dates, numbers and everything.

I do not remember today much in the way of the details of what I learned in Kennedy School. But what I am still using today is the analytical way of addressing issues. That is very important … applicability, applicability."

Me adding: "Learning that stays with you. Did your professors or fellow students ever needle or make fun of you because they knew you were a rising star … otherwise your government would not have sent you to Harvard?"

"I don't recall that prediction from my professors, but [here he hesitates] back then students regarded me as a kind of assistant professor. They knew that I came from the Korean government and when they were talking about international affairs, then they wanted to get my viewpoint. So they nicknamed me the assistant professor."

"Was the perspective of the Harvard professors significantly more internationalist than the Korean ones?"

"Oh, yes, I think so. One of the great strengths of the Kennedy School is that they focused on real politics."

"You mean less model building."

"Less academic, more future-oriented and analytical and sometimes we were given actual subjects … events or problems happening at that time and we were asked to write a memo as if you were an assistant to the president of the United States."

"As to what would you do?"

"Like, what would you recommend in just two pages? This was difficult to write!"

"Oh I know."

"Harder than writing 10 pages. That kind of practical exercise really helped me to understand and also to strengthen my capacity as a future diplomat. Later I overheard students talking that one day Ban would become foreign minister."

"You really loved Harvard, didn't you?"

He agrees with that. Ban enrolled in a number of courses but his favorite was "The Practice of Diplomacy". It was co-taught by two professors (stars back then, and stars now) of Harvard: Graham Allison and Joseph Nye. The former is a world-respected nuclear arms and proliferation expert and the latter is, perhaps, best known for his persuasive articulation of the concept of 'soft power'.

Ban confirming: "At the Kennedy School, I really liked the class on diplomacy. I was told that a U.S. president would never read any memo longer than two pages, so however complex the issue, whatever the difficult issue may be, I should write a memo in two pages. Everything, background, policy options, recommendations…"

"Right. Boom, boom, boom."

"Yes."

"Now, do you make your staff do that?"

"At the UN, yes, I've been trying to do that. There are so many long, long reports. As secretary general, of course I do not have any power to dictate what UN member states do. But they would present very thick, long reports, then you have to translate these documents into six official languages. It costs a lot of money, so what I did is that, however thick it may be, with all documents, there should be a summary report. Thirteen pages. Maximum 13 pages. In 12 font size. Longer than 13 pages, we will not translate it into official languages; then for the summary report, we will translate only that into the six official languages. Other than that, we will translate into only English and French, only two languages — what we call working languages. There are two working languages: English, French. Official languages, according to alphabetical order, [are] Arabic, Chinese, English, French, Russian and Spanish."

You have to laugh. Having attended college at Amherst and graduate school at Princeton on the east coast, and having taught classes for many years at Loyola Marymount University and UCLA, I can report authoritatively that seeing the term 'efficiency' and 'university' in the same sentence is a rare treat indeed. But here you have it — and the credit for this breakthrough has to go to the Harvard Kennedy School, of all places!

GETTING SACKED

Back in South Korea, at a high point in his career as a diplomat, before he went to the UN, Ban was often dubbed "the slippery eel" (a rough and unflattering translation from Korean). The knock was that getting a straight answer out of this polished career diplomat would take the intervention of a sadistic dentist using a patient chair that had a locked steel seatbelt. But when I mentioned an interview I'd had in 2002 with the late President Kim Dae-jung at the Blue House, it was Ban who volunteered the recollection of his career low point — the day when he was fired by the South Korean president himself.

"As you may know, one day I was sacked from the vice ministership of foreign affairs. Then the president was Kim Dae-jung, who had a difficult relationship with U.S. President George Bush."

That is putting it delicately.

Often U.S.-South Korean relations seem parallel lines that never meet. You get a pro-sunshine Korean president, then you got an anti-sunshine American president; you got an anti-sunshine Korean president, now you get a pro-sunshine US president.

But when George W. Bush took office as the 49th president of the U.S., he wasn't going anywhere near Korea, north or south. He arrived with a strong predisposition to believe the worst of the Nobel Prize-winning efforts to keep North Korea engaged in diplomacy through the diplomatic device of the 'Sunshine Policy' of engagement.

That so-called policy of 'sunshine' is founded on the optimistic assumption that diplomacy itself can avoid the worst. For his unstinting efforts, the late Kim Dae-jung was awarded the Nobel Peace Prize in 2000. Alas, at this writing, North Korea seems no closer to normality than ever. But many Koreans admired Kim's commitment to the diplomatic process and resented the new American president's brusque dismissal of that approach.

W — the media shorthand for the younger Bush, less respected than the older, the 41st U.S. president — was instinctively skeptical of negotiations. But the very worried and somewhat stubborn DJ (nickname for the Korean leader) insisted on an early White House meeting to work out misunderstandings, even though the Blue House was warned that pushing the equally stubborn Bush might prove counterproductive.

I ask Ban how he would describe that March 2001 White House session between Kim and Bush Jr.

"Disaster!"

I laugh, but of course that is the perfect word.

"Did he blame you for that?"

"He blamed me, knowing that I was the vice minister regarded as the American hand and expert in the U.S.-Korean relationship. One day, without any notice, I was just fired."

"After that terrible meeting."

"That's right."

"Now did you tell him not to go or to go? Or was he going, no matter what you said? Was he right to blame you or was he just looking for a scapegoat?"

"This is a complicated story. When President Bush was elected, President Kim Dae-jung was very uneasy and he really wanted to see the new U.S. government continue the same relationship and policy regarding North Korea…"

Sunshine policy.

"…as Clinton did. And he wanted to be the first [foreign] president to visit the U.S. But we were advised by the new Bush administration team to wait, as the new administration was reviewing all policies. They said we are fully aware of your concerns, we are reviewing the North Korean policy, and it will take six months. But we insisted. After all, our own president was, by that time, a Nobel Peace Laureate and he had such a distinguished leadership record. And he insisted that he should meet President Bush before you Americans finalize your North Korean policy. Very reluctantly, then, the new Bush government invited him early ... early March."

"It was March and our new president Bush didn't know what he was doing."

"Ahh..." is all he says.

Here, there is a diplomatic pause. His critics would say here, the eel was darting for cover amid dense sea grass.

Ban recalls ruefully: "Well, Bush asked very direct questions before the U.S. media cameras, after the summit meeting. Then when they were having the joint press conference, Bush just—"

"I wrote in a column at the time that Bush was very rude to Dae-jung."

"Yes, yes, quite rude. That became scandalous..."

"Back home."

"...scandalous back at home. So then President Kim Dae-jung's image was very tarnished, and the March summit was a total diplomatic failure. He was very unhappy and so he decided to fire me and before that he also fired the foreign minister. So both the foreign minister and the vice foreign minister were fired."

Ban says this almost without emotion. Sometimes one imagines this Korean gentleman almost defining the phrase "he's an adult".

"For me, as a career diplomat, being the vice minister should not have been the end. I should have been posted somewhere as ambassador but I was totally sacked and became just a private citizen."

"Just like that?"

"Yes. It was just unprecedented."

Me pushing: "DJ was insistent on getting into the White House. Did anybody say maybe that's not a good idea?"

Ban takes that one carefully: "My suggestion was that we needed to have more ground work … to slow it down, to slow it down … groundwork."

"Why did you feel that?"

"Because we knew that there was a total difference of approach on some issues between the Clinton and Bush administrations."

I do believe his version of what happened.

"And so I thought it would be a little bit premature."

"Right, and you know American politics. When the new guy comes in, he wants to do things differently from the other guy."

Ban gets up and moves to refill my teacup — mine first, of course, then his own.

"There was one other diplomatic scandal that added to the problem. It was when Russian President Putin visited South Korea just before President Bush was inaugurated. The South Korean government and Russian government had issued a joint statement where we agreed to a clause about the ABM Treaty that exactly repeated what President Clinton and the Russian government had signed."

Me agreeing: "Big mistake." The Bush crowd loved the idea of putting anti-missile systems around Russia, whether Russia liked it or not — and maybe especially if it didn't.

"Yes, it was a big mistake, but the joint statement was an exact quotation from the U.S.-Russia joint statement, signed by President Clinton."

"But then came the Neocons…" They had just gotten into power.

"Right … well, *The New York Times* carried all this as if we South Koreans were moving closer to the Russian Federation, which infuriated the Bush people."

"They were generally a mean bunch, easy to infuriate."

Ban ignores that too: "This question was raised to President Kim Dae-jung repeatedly: 'Are you intending to come closer to the position of the Russian Federation, etc.?' And because of that I was held politically responsible."

"It has never been my experience that the top guy blames himself, he always blames someone below him."

But how did Ban rise from the dead?

He credits Dr. Han Seung-soo.

"I had a very good relationship with him. Former Prime Minister Roh Shin-young and former Prime Minister Han Seung-soo … they were sort of mentors. Dr. Han then took me with him to the United Nations when he was elected president of the General Assembly. So I was reinstated."

"Rehabilitated!" This was for the 56th General Assembly in 2001.

He smiles: "Yes, rehabilitated, that was the beginning of my small luck. Then, when I came back after serving one year as chief of staff for the president of the General Assembly, there was a change of government from DJ to Roh Moo-hyun, you know, our former president who committed suicide."

"The Korean president who adored the Abe Lincoln story and who wanted to be the Korean Lincoln."

"Yes, he liked the Lincoln life story. I was totally unknown to him but somehow my name was mentioned among others as a potential foreign minister. But the catchphrase in Korea at the time was participatory government … the aim was for real democracy, participatory democracy."

"I see, almost like e-government."

"Right, and so a lot of names must have been generated and I must have been one of them, and according to rumor, my name was the number one choice from the general public."

"What about the elite?"

"Elite, like journalists?"

I laugh: "No, like professors."

"Professors, government officials and some foreign ministry staff at random … some felt that I should have been appointed as first foreign minister of the new Roh administration, but I was not selected and some totally new unknown professor was appointed, who had been working as campaign advisor on diplomacy. He was Professor Yoon, who was nine years junior to me and in the same Seoul National University I attended, and taught international relations. But he became the foreign minister and I became diplomatic advisor to President Roh."

"Sent to the Blue House?"

"In the Blue House for the second time!" The first time was as diplomatic advisor to the former President Kim Young-sam, in 1996.

"Back to that job."

"Back to that job!" The formal title is presidential foreign policy advisor. The U.S. equivalent is national security advisor. This was in 2003.

"It was totally unexpected and, in fact, I declined at first when it was offered. I had a similar job almost eight years ago, so I wanted to be ambassador somewhere   preferably the UN   my specialty. I asked, 'What about if you send me to New York as the UN ambassador?' They said, well, this one is an important job, many people recommended you as foreign minister but somebody has already been designated, so there is no possibility for you. But if you work hard, there may be a possibility. This is what the then chief of staff to the president told me, so I decided to accept that offer and I worked for 10 months as national security advisor to the president. Then, the relationship between President Roh and President Bush was very very   "

"Negative."

"Strained, well, yes … negative. And he'd been publicly criticizing President Bush and he was outspoken, and Western media nicknamed him a maverick. Then our relationship was bad, and our then foreign minister had a very serious quarrel with Colin Powell."

POWELL TELEPHONES

Ban gives the background: President Bush wanted Korea to dispatch Korean forces to Iraq as a member of the anti-Saddam coalition. But the Korean president was opposed.

Understandably. "The famous coalition of the unwilling." Sorry, I have to laugh. What a really bad joke that war was.

"So our president instructed our foreign minister that if the Americans keep pressing strongly, then you should give it to them with conditionality. At that, U.S. Secretary of State Colin Powell was very angry. *We are allies, we don't work that way*, he said. *We fought in the Korean War without any preconditions, you are now presenting preconditions...* It went on like this. Then our foreign minister sent over by courier a book [*Defense Policy Choices for the Bush Administration 2001–2005*] written by an American scholar that was critical of Bush. The scholar's name was Michael O'Hanlon."

"From the Brookings Institution."

"Right!"

"He said: 'Why don't you read this book?' That really provoked the anger of Colin Powell. 'I know all about this book,' he said."

Remember: Powell was, relatively speaking, the 'good guy' in the Bush administration.

"As all these things were happening, there were serious problems among the Korean foreign ministry staff — the rise of a so-called contempt against the presidency. They were ridiculing the Korean president and this was reported to Roh, who was so angry that he fired the foreign minister. Then I was appointed. Now, looking back, had I been appointed as the first, I might have been the one fired! I might have been fired because of all this controversy!"

"You were the second wave!"

"Right. And the Americans were happy with my appointment because they found somebody with whom they could communicate. And Colin Powell was happy. He telephoned me from Washington even before I got the official letter of appointment."

"Is that right?"

"What did he say, do you remember?"

"Oh, he was very happy, he gave me his congratulations. He said he regarded the U.S.-Korea relationship as very important and he was happy to have somebody that is a good friend of America now working as his counterpart. This is something he told me! That, I say, is luck."

"That's luck."

"That's luck."

"Timing is everything in life."

"Timing is everything. Otherwise, I would've already been gone from the Korean Foreign Service and I would not have become UN secretary general."

Harvard Professors on Ban Ki-moon

In the 1980s Ki-moon, then in his thirties, studied at Harvard's John F. Kennedy School of Government on a Korean government fellowship. Here are two accounts of what the future UN secretary general was like back then.

PROFESSOR GRAHAM ALLISON

One of the best anecdotes from his association with the Kennedy School and me is this: I was the "Founding Dean" of the School when he showed up. In one of the early years, the class was quite small. I welcomed them all at an opening reception that included a receiving line where I shook hands with and chatted with each of the new students. When he got to the front of the line, he introduced himself as "JFK". I reacted with predictable surprise. He responded "just from Korea". Thereafter, among his classmates, he was nicknamed JFK.

He was a student in one of my courses. I saw him from time to time while he was a student here. I have kept in touch with him, including when he was foreign minister in Korea and in his present role where my former Executive Director, Bob Orr, is now working for him as an assistant secretary general.

I suspect that he has told you the story of another connection between him and JFK, namely when he visited the White House and saw President Kennedy. When he became secretary general, I suggested to Teddy Kennedy that he might get from the JFK Library a copy of the photo from that event and the comments JFK gave. He did, and Ban Ki-moon keeps it as a valuable reminder.

PROFESSOR JOSEPH NYE

I remember him as a student but not the details of his performance. With 10,000 students over the years, I can no longer recover that degree of detail. But I saw him when he was in the Blue House [as presidential foreign policy advisor] and I was in the Pentagon [as an assistant secretary of defense in the Clinton administration]. Those were difficult times with North Korea, and I thought Ban Ki-moon was a voice of reason. As for his job as secretary general, friends tell me he has done better in practice than the press accounts. One of the problems with that job is the unreasonable public expectation for a role that has limited power.

ANTICIPATED SPEARS WOUND LESS.

– Utopia

Asian Workaholic

**No respect ... power not eternal ...
how they lie ... Ban and Israel**

GIVEN THE TORTURED warrior past between Japan and Korea, is it noteworthy that perhaps Ban Ki-moon's favorite restaurant in Manhattan is Japanese?

There we were at Nippon, the quiet, nicely understated establishment on East 52nd Street. It is seven blocks from the South Korean mission to the United Nations, where Ban had once served years ago while grinding to the top of the Korean foreign service. Restaurants, like friends and allies, the UNSG honors almost religiously.

At that very restaurant he had once asked for my views on what he should do at the UN. This was shortly after he was installed as Kofi Annan's successor, and I had to laugh over that. What did I really know? But I gave him one anyway, because I had one recommendation, on a subject I might arguably be qualified to assess.

I said something like: Get an outside media-image team to come in and work you up to be as bulletproof as possible from the U.S. media.

"Why?" he had asked, looking puzzled.

"They will eat you up, take bites out of your flesh, if you don't give them a lot of razzmatazz. Honestly, this is what will happen."

He arched his eyebrows. He was surprised. He assumed the secretary general of the UN would be accorded dignity.

You had to wonder where his naïveté about the media came from.

"Their appetite is insatiable, so you have to figure out how to feed them. If you don't, you go on the main-course menu."

Ban replied that he wanted to be judged by his hard work and record of accomplishment.

"That may be what you want, but that is not how it always works, especially in New York."

Ban listened but he did not say anything. Nor did he wind up doing anything extra about his media image. And so he was almost eaten alive during the first half or so of the first term. Totally predictable — and possibly preventable.

And so when he strolled into the Secretariat in January 2007 as the new boss of bosses, his prospects were immediately handicapped by a tepid and hostile environment. Our strung-out news media always requires charisma fixes, and in the department of overt charisma Ban was not exactly top-grade heroin. The result was that Ban seemed to have no friends or allies other than the small palace guard of Koreans who surrounded him like blocking American football linemen.

He looks back to the bleak initial days: "Of course, it's better now. I'm quite widely known by this time. But people were comparing me with my predecessor from day one."

The hurt is obvious.

"I thought it was not fair because comparing somebody who has been here for 10 years as secretary general of the UN to someone who has just been elected, and who was just foreign minister of South Korea ... Then it is quite natural that I would be known less ... That was not balanced."

Fair? When has the news media ever been determined to be fair? Where has he been living?

Alas, the poor (or non-existent) outside performance reviews by even responsible print media intensified Ban's me-against-them isolation in year one — and reinforced the Korean diplomat's penchant for paranoia. He began to feel that all the building's bureaucrats were against him. And many, in fact, were, as they might be with any intruding alien force, especially a new SG; and those who were neutral simply had no reason to stick their heads out from their office cubbyholes in support. Certainly he was getting scant outside media help to fluff up an image of some Asian whirlwind that would sweep you away if you got in the way. In fact, a March edition of *Newsweek* flatly predicted he would fail — so stated on its cover!

The early months were horrible, lonely, frustrating. At the office he was moody and sometimes even over the top with anger. His Korean-national staff knew him well enough to duck, be humble and take it in stride. But the UN careerists who didn't know Korean from kosher were stunned, put-off, angry … wary.

The home front was bumpy. The ordinarily stoic and self-contained Soon-taek would go mum, knowing intuitively that things at the office were not exactly peachy. She could read that on her husband's face. The promised house on the East River with the extra bedrooms for the grandchildren, whose visits flooded her heart with tides of love, was months behind schedule. They made their new home in the hotel residence suite provided by the UN, which might have delighted almost anyone, except a real grandmother with real grandchildren who needed some real space.

Sometimes Mrs. Ban was given to slipping out of the hotel in desperation. This would be when the bored UN security team was off getting coffee and sandwiches. All but disguised in the tasteful but plain-looking clothes that are her constant modest preference, she would steal away for an afternoon by her lonesome self in a darkened foreign-film movie theater, until the security boys caught onto her game.

Their mutual misery only started to ease when the townhouse was finally done (maybe Rome went up faster?) and her new full life could begin. And it eased as Ban began to contain that Kumkang mountain temper and focus his enormous energies and career-confirmed competence on the doable rather than the dreamed of.

NO RESPECT

Especially early on, though, it did sometimes seem as if Ban Ki-moon, career diplomat, got too little respect. Vicious and cruel dictators would sometimes practically laugh to themselves when he'd telephone privately from his Secretariat office in New York to read them the human-rights 'riot act', imploring them to respect their citizens rather than shoot them. This would seem like an eminently sensible request but, for a confirmed and cruel dictator, it must have come across as a call for wimpy total disarmament or something. Ban, like the other pope, the Catholic one, has at his immediate command no combat divisions, of course. Perhaps he'd prefer to have a few on hand to shake in a dictator's face when moral justice might require. But, somehow, the member states haven't gotten round to adding that to the repertoire of the options for the UNSG.

Then there's the feared UN bureaucracy. All bureaucracies everywhere — at almost any level of government, in virtually every country and in every culture, from Venezuela to the Vatican — resent and resist the Hot-Shot New Guy coming in. The sole exception is when the new guy on the block comes in with a machine gun ... What was it that Machiavelli said about the difference between being feared or loved?

But it has to be said that the resistance to his ideas and reforms, even the simplest ones, from the deeply embedded Secretariat bureaucracy was especially fierce and ungracious, certainly in the first years of his first term.

He had little ammunition with which to counterattack. Even his fellow Koreans, though rightly proud that one of theirs was awarded the coveted job of the world's top diplomat, quietly deplored his lack of charisma and inelegance in spoken English. The French were put out — but aren't they always, by something or other? — by the Korean man's inelegant French, a language option asked of any SG out of a sense of UN tradition. Well, the tradition ought to be retired, but Ban tried hard, for a while giving up hours every Saturday to take French-language lessons.

Had he been from a different cut of cloth, Ban might have been destroyed by it all. Now in his mid-sixties, the former South Korean foreign minister was certainly well aware of the unrelenting negative drumbeat around him; in fact, it had been deeply painful.

There was even a time or two in his first term when the always calm and gentle Soon-taek, his loving wife of four decades, would read his mind and suffer with him the unspoken and unspeakable thought that maybe it had all been a mistake, that the job of 'secular pope', widely described as a truly impossible job for mere mortals, was not for him, and that a second term was not only not on the cards but in fact was a distinctly questionable idea both for his health and sanity.

After all, how many belts could one man take, even a tough Korean man?

But they do turn out their Koreans tough, whether it's yesteryear's woman about to give birth and wondering whether she's seeing her shoes for the last time (see "Looking Down at Their Shoes" on pages 145–151) or the world's top diplomat questioning whether he can pull this whole UN thing off or is he just hitting his head against a brick wall.

He got hot over either outright rejection or passive resistance. Aides noticed that he was especially disturbed by the lack of respect, if not for him personally, at least for the office itself. He could barely contain his anger.

But a major part of the problem may have been Ban himself.

I ask, now well into his fourth year: "I have a theory about you. In South Korea, the foreign minister in that hierarchical Korean culture is the top dog, and in the foreign ministry if he says everyone goes left, everyone goes left!"

He nods.

"And if he says everyone goes right, everyone goes right."

"That's right. That is a very good point."

But that is not the case at the UN Secretariat.

"The first year, there were, I think, some misunderstandings about me. You know, I'm only the second Asian secretary general after U Thant. That took 36 years, so there was not much Asian thinking or Asian values appreciated within the UN system. Those people who had been working with U Thant, in his time, they have all disappeared. Since then, UN people have been mostly working with European and Latin American approaches, and Kofi Annan almost reflected a European way of thinking. Even though he comes from

> You know, I'm only the second Asian secretary general after U Thant. That took 36 years, so there was not much Asian thinking or Asian values appreciated within the UN system.

Africa, he spent almost 40 years within UN system, and he was educated mainly in Europe and the U.S., and he was living with a European wife as a spouse, and so, he was from a predominantly European, Western culture.

"Of course, I have been educated and raised in a largely Confucian atmosphere, even though at this time in South Korea the young generation, they are totally different, but at least in my generation people have been brought up and educated in such a way so it has been embedded in my body ... But at the same time I'm one of the few South Koreans maybe who have been exposed to Western culture over time, so I know both cultures well and I'm able to adapt myself to both. But even with that, when I first became secretary general and started dealing with so many multicultural, multilateral, multi-ethnicities, well, that was quite the challenge. My predecessors came from Western cultures and I'm only the second Asian secretary general — one who spent most of my time in Korea."

One of his first successes, completed early on, was splitting off the administrative from the operational duties of the UN's sprawling peacekeeping empire. When the binary structure was finally in place, many agreed the move was justified. But still there had been opposition anyhow. He was always being tested: *Get the Korean!* Even so, he was starting to get traction. As the oft-repeated Korean saying goes: What doesn't kill you makes you stronger.

We all know the feeling at the outset: *Will I be accepted, rejected? Ignored?*

Me saying: "The first year of any job is horrible. I don't care whether you're running the Boy Scouts of America or serving fries at McDonald's, or in the White House. I mean, the first year, I never sleep. You don't sleep anyhow, but that's another issue. But you've grown into it, haven't you? Talk a little bit about how."

The green tea is on the table and we reach for our cups at the same time. It is raining in New York like a movie set filming the end of the world. In classical Korean style, the secretary general lifts my cup and saucer with two hands, and I receive it with two hands as well.

He says it was pretty horrible when he first came in.

"The members?"

"In particular [staff officials] in the Secretariat. Because they were not, uh, accustomed to Asian values, and there were no senior level Asian people working in the Secretariat. You know, Japan and China were holding one or two important senior posts but otherwise there have not been many Asians. That was a difficulty.

"I really wanted to bring some dynamism, some change of thinking, some discipline, some accountability and ethics to the United Nations system. That was resisted very strongly by the existing members of the system."

He sips tea and stares at me for what seems like the longest time.

"But in the end, during the last four and a half years, I think they now understand, clearly, that Asian values are also one of the very important values, and cultures, which should be respected, and Asian countries, like Korea, China, India and Japan — you know, Japan has always been there — they're doing well now. And that's why people have been saying that the 21st century will be led by the Asia-Pacific."

"And you agree with that?"

"Yes, yes. I agree with that. Take the example of Singapore. They have shown good values, good models from Asia."

He shakes his head: "The general understanding in the Western world is that people tend to believe that whatever has been the tradition or culture of the West is something to be practiced by all other people. There is some [room for] conflict with that, and the UN is the place where you can see all these different cultures, so all these different cultures should be respected as such. Korean culture is also one of the important cultures, and I wanted to keep some of my culture. At least part of the Korean success story should be something that needs to be emulated: Koreans have been successful in developing good governance. I really wanted to bring that kind of best practice to the United Nations and, in fact, I made some progress in that, so now, people understand."

> I really wanted to bring some dynamism, some change of thinking, some discipline, some accountability and ethics to the United Nations system. That was resisted very strongly by the existing members of the system.

Even if they didn't like Koreans or didn't like him and his ways, or didn't think he was one of them, was he not in fact the occupier of the most prestigious diplomatic job on earth? Where was their sense of respect for the UN, if not for the man in the seat at the time?

"Have you been on American TV very much?"

"Not much. Sometimes CNN, PBS ... I think, once or twice each. ABC, NBC, CBS, like that."

"You've been on Al Jazeera probably more, right?"

"Oh yes, Al Jazeera, more."

"You know who gives you good media coverage? The only network in my opinion that gives you good coverage is Al Jazeera ... of course they are very international."

Ban chuckles: "And because I have been exerting my time and energy and my passion on improving the relationship between Israel and Arab countries and Palestinians. When I was trying to draw out an armistice ceasefire between them, I traveled to four countries a day. That was real shuttle diplomacy. I was going from early morning, flying to create political atmosphere so that pressure would be felt by the Israeli government. Finally I was able to draw them out into a ceasefire." This was in 2009.

Ban adding: "Even so, U.S. media seem to be not much interested in the United Nations, and that's what I feel a bit ... it's strange sometimes, and it's not fair to Americans, who are paying 22 percent of the cost of the UN every year."

"But if you look at all the polls, Americans seem in general to approve of the UN."

"Well, this is not a complaint, but do you know how much they carried, the *New York Times*, the *Wall Street Journal*, when I was re-elected?"

"I was amazed. It was almost nothing."

"Is that not news?"

"I was surprised." Just two years ago, it might have been totally unexpected news, with rumors that he might be a one-term UNSG, like the Egyptian Boutros Boutros-Ghali (1992–1996).

Ban saying: "I was shocked. I was shocked."

I say: "It is almost a non-event, a big story in only a few places, such as *China Daily*, which I actually subscribe to. Maybe you're a bigger deal in China than you are in America?! The *Wall Street Journal* was the only one that had something. It's like the only news is bad news, and you weren't news by that definition. Maybe that's not so bad!"

He shakes off the attempt at wit: "They're not paying much attention to the United Nations. Simply, the importance and seriousness of what the United Nations is doing is much more important than what, you know, local news often carries."

"Do you get to see Al Jazeera television very much? What do you think of it?"

He nods and smiles: "Al Jazeera has become one of the most influential news media. I have had many interviews with Al Jazeera, and when it comes to certain situations in the region I think they are the best. They are most informed, well aware of the situation and how it develops, so it's very important. If I don't see it a certain day, on a certain important subject, there are many UN staff who watch Al Jazeera, and the first thing I do in my office is that I get briefings from my spokesperson who collects all the news. He starts working at 4am. He collects all the important news and brings it to me, so every day he's the first person I meet."

> When I was trying to draw out an armistice ceasefire between them [Israel, Arab countries and Palestinians], I traveled to four countries a day. That was real shuttle diplomacy … so that pressure would be felt by the Israeli government. Finally I was able to draw them out into a ceasefire.

"When is that meeting, usually? What time of day?"

"Eight forty-five or nine o'clock, or … but, as soon as I get up, I check my e-mail. He sends all to my e-mail, so I first see all the headlines. By reading them, I understand."

"You can make sense of it?"

"Good sense."

"So, Al Jazeera's really filled a gap, and let's face it, the Western media has been good on some issues, but not good on others. And Al-jazz also gives a balance on the Israel Question … which has got to be one of the toughest issues for you."

Ban agreeing: "That would be one of the tense and tough issues of any year … how to deal with the Israeli and Palestinian relationship."

POWER NOT ETERNAL

"Even Lee Kuan Yew had to step down after a long time?"

"Oh, yes. Nobody is eternal. I've been telling Mugabe of Zimbabwe the Korean saying: *No flower lasts longer than 10 days.* But of course there are some people ... for them there is no reasonable period of time.

"It is very disappointing [he coughs], I have seen quite a number of [coughs a bit more intensely again and reaches for some tea] such leaders. Foolishly, they believe that [puts cup down] the power they enjoy at this time will be eternal."

"That's a pretty good line ... power is not eternal."

"My straight message to these leaders in my private talks is, 'Mr. President, you have to leave your legacy as a president who has been committed to democratization of your country. How long do you think you can go on like this? Power is not eternal. You will someday have to leave your office, so just cling to this power by doing that [repression]? What is more important is your eternal legacy after you leave office.' That has been my earnest straightforward advice to those people. But I often hear from wise people that when you are in power then sometimes you are blinded."

"Maybe like a drug."

"I don't know about that but you are blinded. You are surrounded by all these people who really..."

"Yes Men."

"Right. Because of that you are blinded, whether you want to be or not. That's very sad but in this 21st century, there are still many people who cling to power, sometimes trying to change their constitutions when they are not eligible for a third term. They just want to change the limitation, and while you are in the office of the president, it can sometimes be done. That kind of thing has created a lot of tensions."

Me saying: "When you see someone who is in this self-regarding bubble, the eternal maximum leader or semi-divine king or whatever — do you just say this guy is hopeless, or are you the eternal optimist and do you say I'm going to try to punch through the bubble, give them a reality check?"

"I want to offer some political wisdom to explain why power is not eternal."

"Yeah, power is not eternal."

"Yeah, power is not eternal. What is more important is your eternal legacy. Leave your legacy in a good way and that's what I have been telling them."

But if power is not eternal for the tyrant who'd stay forever and a day, what about the workaholic who gives the job 101 percent? Does she or he go on forever?

I note: "Someone said to me, 'Ban Ki-moon's going to run for the presidency of South Korea after his 10 years as secretary general of the UN.' I said, 'No, Ban Ki-moon's going to rest.'"

He laughs in clear delight: "You are right. You do know me! You're right!"

"He's going to write his memoirs, he's going to spend a lot

of time with his wife and his grandchildren, make some nice speeches…"

Yes, indeed, says his body language: "I know what kind of quality I have. I'm a born diplomat. Politics? I think there are many other people who can really be engaged in national politics. This job, the position of secretary general may look like a political one. Yes, of course, I have to deal with many political issues…"

> 💬 Yeah, power is not eternal. What is more important is your eternal legacy. Leave your legacy in a good way and that's what I have been telling them. 💬

"Right."

"…very sensitive, international political issues, but this is diplomacy. Diplomacy's often called an art, balancing different positions among many different players."

Me saying: "You know, when you think of Asian values, in the context of your job, you could say that Asian values seek a balance between group responsibility and the individual — looking for balance, rather than going one way or the other. Are Asian values one aspect of your desire to be fierce about finding the doable middle ground, what you can really achieve, as opposed to entirely pleasing one party or the other?"

"I'm a very realistic person, and I don't think I'm such a big idealist. I'm very practical, and that is what I've been asking of the parties … to really be flexible and practical, and try to meet at the middle point. You cannot get 100 percent. The maximum is 60 percent, 70 percent, or even 80 percent. But, still, when you get 80 percent..."

"Eighty percent would be terrific."

He doesn't agree: "If you leave only 20 percent [for the other party or parties], that can become another source of conflict and distrust. When you can have a reasonably good balance between the two conflicting parties, I think that can be called a success. You cannot have 100 percent success. That is domination, or occupation, or hegemony."

"That would be the Leviathan model of secretary general."

"Yeah, that's right."

"And that's a fiction, isn't it? That's for the media."

He nods vigorously. "The Leviathan way of thinking is not for the secretary general."

That's a strong and memorable way of putting it.

"Part of the public perception problem is you're just not a natural showboat and so you're kind of hard to get a fix on. The media antenna is basically a blunt instrument; it's not a fine lens you know? I remember you said ... it was off the record but here we are ... A predecessor — let's not name him, you said — would go into a meeting with a national leader where there was a serious issue and they would joke and fool around, and then he would come out and give a press conference and say 'and I really told him off etc. etc.'. But you tell me you're just the opposite, you go in and give them a hard time, and then you come out and say you just had, with so-and-so leader, a frank, pleasant and fruitful exchange of views — a bland statement — whereas inside, you were actually giving him Korean hell. I mean you can't photograph that!"

Ban agrees with all of this, of course.

He laughs at this. "How can the media capture the inner mind? The inner feeling? Or what really went on behind the scenes. For that, perhaps what one requires is very good print journalism."

Me continuing: "Your diplomatic style is a style that actually the camera will always miss … It captures your face, your voice, your gestures and even a bit of your body language … ok. But for the more complex things, the cameras and the media are really inept in capturing that."

Ban: "I am still in the process of improving my style or my leadership capacity, but my leadership style comes from a philosophy of collective leadership. There is a general tendency for people in the international community that they want to have a certain one person coming up with some strong political slogan or belief or leading in a dynamic way in what is termed so-called leadership. But when you run an international organization like this one, the effectiveness of leadership can come only from support from everybody. I'm not a national government leader, or a leader from some developing country where they have almost absolute power, where whatever the president or prime minster thinks can carry the agenda within their national politics.

"Of course, there are always opposition parties and it's not that easy, but when it comes to the United Nations, you have 193 board members and there are five board members who have veto power, then there are divisions of positions between developing countries and developed countries in two large groups, and there are many sub-groups, regional groups, continent-wise, all sorts of sub-regional groups. All these groups play into the UN … therefore how to reconcile differences among all these different groups?

"That really requires a balanced way of coordinating. This is why I have been saying that my leadership will only be strengthened with support not only from my senior advisors but also with support from member states that can be part of my leadership. That is what I have termed as my leadership philosophy and I think I have been more or less successful in managing this style.

"One who is a very strong ego-type person will never be successful in the UN, but if you are too soft you will again not be regarded as a relevant leader. Therefore, how to position the secretary general in this way is really an extraordinarily difficult and sensitive task, but that's what I find myself doing as secretary general."

Of course, he adds: "As now the world's top diplomat, I agree that this diplomatic approach should not always be confined to what is known as quiet diplomacy or behind-the-scenes diplomacy. That is just one part of the diplomatic skill set. There is also public diplomacy … You can always meet your counterpart in a public way, and you can sometimes criticize publicly; and when it comes to universally accepted principles, like human rights, freedom, democracy, sometimes you have to be vocal and you have to state your positions clearly, and convey very clearly not only to the parties in question but also to the whole world, because the whole world should know what the UN is doing."

The secretary general did not say it, but one event to illustrate that approach was his May 2012 appearance in Myanmar. With the opening of the fledgling parliament, Ban gave what was described as a 'historic' speech. It was the first by a foreign dignitary to that parliament. His agreement to appear there helped forge a compromise between Thein Sein's governing party and Aung San Suu Kyi's National League for Democracy party in the effort to get the reform momentum going.

To both, behind the scenes, Ban and his staff urged an end to squabbling over what could be depicted as a technical issue over what constitutes loyal obedience to the Constitution. Later, in his public address, he said this: Put aside your differences and focus on "the longer-term interests of the country and the immediate needs of the people."

This was pure Ban. So was his call for the further easing of trade restrictions and other sanctions on the apparently liberalizing regime.

Ban's general approach, except in instances of absolute principle, is to split the difference if you want to move forward.

"You cannot have it 100 percent your own way. As much as you can maintain your own integrity and your basic positions, there is always room for flexibility. Along these lines one can always have some constructive ambiguity in a way so that you can interpret what was agreed to as meeting your interest and my interest as well.

This is something always seen in the diplomatic world."

"One of the reasons for your second term is that your 'board of directors', the P-5, see how you work. Presumably they understand and accept the Asian style (*reader: think of Donald Trump, then imagine someone exactly the opposite*), and so when the media comes with its rather predictable complaints, it makes it even clearer in their mind that perhaps the professionals really are running the show. Another aspect of your diplomacy that strikes me is the wholesale tolerance of ambiguity."

"Oh, yes, this is sometimes necessary."

Ban explains himself further: "But when universally accepted principles are offended or violated, you have to be very firm, and in an effort to change their attitude, you may engage in very private dialogue. For example, when you talk with a certain leader with many advisors attending the meeting, he or she will tend to show very strong macho-style leadership just to satisfy his own ego and domestic political interests. Then you cannot continue dialogue, especially when somebody is shouting at somebody else."

"And the shouting match hardens positions."

"Yes, it hardens the positions, so there is no way to resolve anything in such a setting. But if you can change the setting and come at it a different way, turn from a just sitting like this — like you and me right now … and speaking humanly and in a sincere way, then I would normally switch and maybe just give my ideas, then ask the leader what should be the best way to address this complex issue, and then I tell them that I will just leave it to you, it would be important for your leadership to solve it, especially vis-a-vis your domestic politics, to show that you have leadership, and so use my ideas as your ideas. And I will not claim authorship. And if you just announce these new policies, then I will only welcome and support your ideas. That will strengthen your domestic politics. I respect your domestic situation, and I do appreciate your domestic pressures.

"I try to engage many leaders in just this way. Then you can always differ but you can continue your dialogue, in public even smiling sometimes, for by that time you understand each other, and I want to avoid causing any public embarrassment. This approach was sometimes misunderstood by Western media or by Western countries, as if I have not been taking any action against dictators or vile perpetrators. But it's not true. It's a total misunderstanding. I have been very vocal with them inside the meeting."

There's no way to know for sure exactly what happens in these closed negotiating sessions, of course.

Ban saying: "So yes, you displease a little all the parties, then they understand the reality. If I satisfy or please only one side, then there will be huge criticism from the other side, regardless of the merit or substance of the issue. But when it comes to fundamental principles, universally accepted principles, we cannot be that way. So there is always some confusion amongst many UN staff."

I ask him to elaborate on what he is said to have proclaimed to close associates: "Neutrality lacks the spirit."

He sees where I am coming from, and responds: "That's why

I've been straightforward. Whether the United Nations is a neutral body, or impartial body, I've been saying the United Nations can never be a neutral organization. Yes, we are impartial. We need to act in an impartial way but we cannot always act in a neutral way. We're not like the Red Cross. We have to sometimes criticize, even though the other party may not like it."

You don't always get to deal with people who you readily approve of, as he implies: "One has lost in the democratic election, one has won this election ... and I have to support the person who was elected democratically, through open and credible election process. So I support. That's the fair and impartial way, true to the principle of democracy."

> I've been saying the United Nations can never be a neutral organization. Yes, we are impartial. We need to act in an impartial way but we cannot always act in a neutral way. We're not like the Red Cross.

Real life presents hard choices.

"But there are many such cases where the values of human rights and democracy collide with development issues. There is an urgent need to help some countries but when a regime is very dictatorial, corrupt, then you have to keep to your principle. This principle — democracy and freedom, and human rights — should prevail over the necessity of economic and social development. So, there is always this kind of balancing issue."

For all his caring about his fellow Korean countrymen in North Korea, in this connection his personal views might be regarded as hawkish by some of his countrymen in the South.

"But in the past, there were problems within the UN systems, where, depending upon the agencies — like development agencies versus human rights or humanitarian agencies — they competed with each other in their own way. So, how to balance all these different agencies, their values and priorities? It is extremely difficult, but as secretary general I have made it quite clear that when these principles or priorities collide, then human rights should prevail over all of them."

"Did they listen?"

"Oh, yes. I made it quite clear."

HOW THEY LIE

"So, you are an adult, you were foreign minister of South Korea and you've been around the block a few times. But when you took this very difficult challenge, one of the things that surprised you was how often people lie to you. It's like a part of the job, being lied to all the time. You once told me you'd been in this business of diplomacy for 40 years but until you got to the UN, you've never been lied to so much."

Tea is replenished and Ban seems to get a second wind: "I try to be as honest as possible, always."

"But when you got to this job, people were lying to you right and left. They would promise x and it would never happen … or something worse would happen."

He almost puts his hand to his head as if he has a headache.

He says to make sure to include cases where leaders pledge money to an agreed good cause, but funds never materialize.

Yet he points out: "Yes, but there are certain cases that, even for me, you promise but you may not be able to keep it because of the situation, inevitably."

"You mean, it comes with the territory."

"Then, that's not a lie."

"Change of circumstances?"

"Change of circumstances. But there are some who tell some stories which, from the beginning, were not true. Well, that's not acceptable."

"But you have to deal with these people."

"This world is not like what I want or you want to believe. You have to deal with many different types of people."

"Is Syria's Assad there in the top five list as one of the worst liars?"

"I think by far he's the—"

"Number one?"

"Number one."

I ask if the real big-time liars are all the same.

He shakes his head.

> So, how to balance all these different agencies, their values and priorities ... It is extremely difficult, but as secretary general, I have made it quite clear that when these principles or priorities collide, then human rights should prevail over all of them.

"Not Gaddafi. When he said he would do something, he tried to do something. Like when I asked him to help find some of our hostages from those kidnappers with whom he would have influence, he instructed his people, look, try to help the secretary general. Let us try to use all our influence. This was with an ambassador who was working for the United Nations; he was kidnapped, and he was released. Sometimes he kept his promise, but he did not keep his promise to his people. That's why he was brutally killed."

Ban continuing: "Now consider Omar-al-Bashir, the Sudanese president. Yes, he's not been keeping his word." The SG shakes his head, reaches for the tea. It's perhaps a very good thing for world peace, not to mention his staff, that he doesn't often reach for anything stronger!

"During the second term, I'll try to be more assertive in some ways because on many occasions, dealing with these dictators … I'm disappointed. I had been addressing them in a very genuine, very humble way, but sometimes they don't keep their word."

"You mean they lied to you?"

It may be that he believes lying to any secretary general is a profound moral wrong.

"Yeah, they lied to me. When they were heavily criticized, publicly, sometimes there were some leaders who would change their ways, but far from all. So sometimes, I thought, all this kind of sincere personal advice, private advice, might not work well."

This is the criticism of Ban in some quarters: He's too quiet a man.

"But I still believe in the usefulness and effectiveness of private talks with leaders, as a diplomat who has been in this business longer than 40 years. But there is not only private diplomacy, which I have been employing, you know. I've now been speaking publicly, too. I've been depending on public as well as private diplomacy. I'll try for a more balanced mix."

He empties the teacup, and rings for more.

"This is one thing, and second, I have to think about my own sustainability ... of my health, or whether I can continue this way, and I have to widen — this is self criticism — my vision or even my personal life. I have not been able to widen my scope to other worlds, like music, or art and sports, which can really enrich my life."

I have to say that on those handful of social occasions I've shared with the Bans — not UN functions, but purely social, to relax — they have indeed been relaxed, and did really enjoy the break from routine, like the rest of us. He likes watching and playing soccer, too, and even injured his hand recently.

One night, in Manhattan, at the Oak Room (since demolished by the corporate management of the once exquisite Algonquin Hotel), we listened to American show tunes, well rendered indeed by a terrific trio and singer. Then there was an intermission break, and when the little stage lights came back on to start act two, the singer asked the audience (mostly loving couples) to recognize and applaud a special VIP: "Ladies and gentlemen, the secretary general of the United Nations!" Delighted, Ban quickly stood up, took a happy bow, and as he sat down and the applause trickled down, some wise guy was heard to shout: "That means no fighting!" I'd never seen Ban smile so much or laugh so hard.

BAN AND ISRAEL

"But what about R2P, Responsibility to Protect [see pages 123–126]. After all, you've got Israel, an ally of the US, and everybody knows about that."

"I don't think this R2P is something to be applied to that."

"You don't?"

"I don't. Israel is willing to protect its own people."

"Yeah, their own people."

"And it's not about genocide. The Israeli state was the outcome of victimization by genocide, mass genocide, crimes by Hitler against humanity. So they know all this, and they support R2P. Now, what I said about R2P is that when the country, or the leader, is not capable of protecting their own people from these crimes against humanity — ethnic cleansing, genocide, war crimes — then the international community should intervene. These days, what this Libyan case has been telling us, and the Syrian case, is that some leaders are not willing to protect their own people. Rather than willing to protect, they are killing their own people, using all heavy weapons. That is why the Security Council has taken very decisive action [on Libya]. It's regrettable that nothing has been decided on

Syria because of the division among permanent members of the Security Council."

(On Saturday, February 4, 2012, another futile Security Council session took place. Only three of the five permanent members voted for the strong resolution calling for Assad to cede power. Opposing were Moscow and Beijing. Afterwards Ban, who — as the New York Times *accurately put it — rarely weighs in on Security Council decisions, called the vote "a great disappointment. It undermines the role of the UN and the international community in this period when the Syrian authorities must hear a unified voice calling for an immediate end to its violence against the Syrian people." He then urged further efforts, whether inside the UN system or outside, to pave the way for a new Syria.)*

"But what do you say to Mahathir, the former Malaysian prime minister, who charges, 'The problem with Ban Ki-moon is he's too close to the Americans on the Israeli issue, and so he doesn't have credibility in the Islamic world.'"

He laughs· "No, I don't agree with that. You will be surprised to see how critical the Israeli media and the Israeli people are of me. Basically, Israelis are against the United Nations, and I have made several difficult choices which were much disliked by Israelis. One was the establishment of a Board of Inquiry on the Gaza war, and the second was the flotilla panel. It's still going on."

"Right." I recall Jim McLay telling me that "everyone thought the flotilla panel idea was dead. But good old Ban," chuckles New Zealand's ambassador to the UN, "quietly chips away, chips away

… never rubbing their noses in it … and gets the Israeli government to accept that its own inquiry would not be credible around the world. So, for the first time, the Israelis agree to be the subject of an outside inquiry."

Ban explaining: "I do not know how many sessions I have spent with Prime Minister Netanyahu, and even the senior leadership of America, like Vice President Biden, or Secretary Clinton, Ambassador Susan Rice, and then the Minister of Defense and Minister of Foreign Affairs from Israel [Lieberman]. I've had a lot of very tough discussions. Finally, I was able to establish this panel on the flotilla. This, they didn't appreciate. They didn't appreciate, but still Israelis respect me, I believe. They respect me because I was doing the right things, and I was not trying to criticize just one side, or offend Israelis without any reason. So it is an unfair assessment that I'm too close to the Americans or to the Israelis, and it is without any cause.

"It is important to also fully understand the genuine concerns of Israeli security. That's what I said, publicly … that I understand. That is why I'm really in support of your cause, to defend you. That's your prerogative, to defend your country and people. Then, what I've been saying to President Shimon Peres — ah, again, I've had a lot of talks with Shimon Peres, and Netanyahu, and all these people. One day, I was talking like this, 'Look, you may choose your friends or your spouse, but you have no choice of your neighbors and your parents. Your neighbors are Arabs and Palestinians, and as long as Israel remains, for many millennia you will have to live harmoniously and peacefully with the Palestinian people.'"

"Right."

"I say: 'You have no choice, and do you really want to have your neighbors always being hostile to you? Can you live that way? Is it sustainable? So for the longer term, you really need an improved relationship with the Palestinians and the whole Arab world. That's your choice for a better future, and I do not want to see your grandchildren, who are not responsible for this current situation, to share this sense of hostility towards each other.' That's what I have been telling them all the time."

"That's another plus of having a South Korean secretary general, because you, as a South Korean, are well-experienced in living with a difficult neighbor."

"Oh, yes, yes."

"With neighbors that you otherwise might not choose to have."

"Until we are united, the South and North Koreas should live peacefully, without any conflict. And so until they are able to have genuine peace in Israel, and the Middle East, they should be able to really negotiate and try to compromise with each other. Israel cannot get 100 percent what it wants, and Arabs vice versa."

That is the philosophy of Ban Ki-moon, which would keep the world out of needless conflicts and moving in better directions … further away from Hobbes and (in all our dreams and wishes) closer to More.

ONE MAN TO LIVE IN PLEASURE AND
WEALTH, WHILE ALL OTHERS WEEP ...
THAT IS NOT THE PART OF A KING,
BUT OF A JAILOR.

– Utopia

The Mandela Marker

**Global not local … R2P … beyond national interest …
UN staff … natural evolution of history …
golden parachute for tyrants?**

THE UN SECRETARY general is just back from a grueling Security Council session. And that was probably the easier part of the day.

There were tense words with an ambassador from the Middle East, the reluctant turn-down of a request for a Sunday morning U.S. network talk-show appearance — as the subject was too hot to talk about in public (he calculates that 20 minutes of "no comments" amid a lackluster stream of generalities/banalities would not enhance the image of the UN, or its SG). And then the personal trip down the hall to what private sector executives would term 'Human Affairs' to find out why not even one single darn female candidate made the recommendations list for the latest high-end opening.

It is now about 4pm and he is standing near the piano, close to a table of VIP-type pictures. But he is not happy. He is eyeing his BlackBerry and scowling. He looks up quickly, then down to the cellphone, maneuvering the dials with the ease of a teenager in the back of the classroom texting with a friend across town. An aide told me that once, in the middle of a session at the 2009 G-20 summit in Pittsburgh, the SG was BlackBerry-ing instructions to a staffer in New York. Multitasking is not a problem for Ban and neither is techie-type stuff, remarkable for a man in his late sixties, which he uses with ease. His predecessor never used e-mails, not to mention BlackBerries. This SG types well and opens attached documents without fuss. But if something goes wrong, he knows who to call and not to fool with the thing himself.

I walk up the stairs and see this scowling scene and find out what's bugging him. It is some self-styled UN critic in a Blog blast (that might have all of just 60 readers) about something or other being wrong with what the UNSG is up to. But he is taking it so seriously — far too seriously.

It could be pointed out that anyone in his position has to expect criticism of all kinds — and from all kinds — and that the higher up you go in the world, the easier it is for the pigeons to hit their mark. But he has to say that to himself. Probably somewhere in his head he knows that. But in his heart he is overly sincere, and that sometimes kills him.

He puts the BlackBerry down, we sit and I ask: "So while we're on the subject, what would be a fair and balanced self-analysis of the first term?"

He knows it is a proper question: "I have been thinking about all this criticism, and some criticism, sometimes, I do not read, not because I don't like to be criticized, but I thought that those criticisms were not fair."

"Unhelpful to you?"

"Not unhelpful … not fair. They were, to my mind, criticizing for the sake of criticism. But at the same time, I often pondered, 'Why are they criticizing me?'"

The answer of course is simple: In part, because he is there, in that job, and in part, because he and his media staff could have done a better job of feeding the beast — the media, with its need for perceptible and reportable surface action.

Me saying: "I think the killer is all those prepared speeches you have to give."

He nods, and adds: "But as secretary general, sometimes you need to be very serious, very formal. I have to read out the text which is written on the basis of all existing UN principles and substantive agendas, but if the occasion becomes more social and more informal then I try to make some effort to deliver off the cuff remarks that I am told can seem more impressive or convincing. There are many different cases. I sometimes make 10 speeches a day … 10!"

"That's too many."

"Big and small."

"That's so many."

"So it is difficult sometimes to read all 10 texts in advance in a short period of time. But you have to digest [the information] and try to present [it] in a really convincing and impressive way. That is one of my challenges that really takes my time."

Sometimes his close personal staff, fearful of their boss falling flat, will recommend a dress rehearsal — on-the-job media training, as it were. He was on a foreign trip when they decided to rehearse the announcement of his candidacy for a second term. They did so in a hotel room, with a podium brought in and all. No more stumbling over words as if he didn't understand them which, of course, he does. The staff itself, putting in 14-hour days routinely, could only take so much. Besides … they did care.

GLOBAL NOT LOCAL

"Now let me add some more about leadership styles. The leaders of our member states are all politicians, but sometimes what you want to see is more statesmen than politicians. Now, there are many politicians, big or small, high or low; but when the politician becomes a nation's leader, then he really needs to be a person who is committed to the global agenda. But, unfortunately, if I view them from the perspective of the secretary general of the United Nations … well, then there is sometimes some conflict between me and them."

"Primarily a big difference in constituencies?"

"Yes, they all have different constituents that are more tied to domestic politics. People say all politics is local and, of course, I can agree, but when they come to the UN, they should come as one of the global leaders, as a member of the UN. They should talk global politics, rather than local politics. That's what I expected."

"But you're not going to get it!"

"Unfortunately, I have not been able to see, here at the UN, many *global* leaders."

"Because they've got other bosses!"

Ban looks at me through those plain wire-rimmed glasses and I honestly think I see pain in his eyes: "That I understand, Tom. But at least when they come to the United Nations, they should try to talk and act and implement as global leaders. Sure, it's natural that all these leaders should have their own personal ego. But personal ego should not be the hurdle preventing them from becoming global statesmen. That does not help one to have sound judgment."

"You mean permanent representatives here to the UN or the big shots back home in their capitals?"

"I mean the [top] leaders. They are all politicians so it's natural they have their own leadership style and ego, but as secretary general of the UN, one can have an ego, but I try to get rid of my personal ego and I try to present myself as just doing public service. Unless I come to global public service as secretary general, I cannot be impartial. Again, that's my commitment, and another perspective on public-service philosophy."

> ...as secretary general of the UN, one can have an ego, but I try to get rid of my personal ego and I try to present myself as just doing public service. Unless I come to global public service as secretary general, I cannot be impartial ... that's my commitment.

He means we have a lonely, threatened, maybe doomed planet when only *one* person can bring a global perspective to the table.

"So your weapon of mass destruction then has got to be the power to shame?"

"More the power to inspire rather than shame."

That's a thought to prompt a pause.

He continues: "Power of persuasion and dialogue with concerned parties. We try to focus on preventive diplomacy, mediation and facilitation. If we can mediate between the conflicting parties, we can prevent war. If we are successful in preventive diplomacy we can prevent war! Now, the tendency of member states is that they are sometimes very generous and swift in paying some 100 million dollars when war or serious conflict of some kind really breaks out, but they are very un-generous if they are asked to pay out a few million dollars for preventive diplomacy. When they don't see the fire, they feel they don't need to spend money. Only after seeing the fire break out will they try to put it out. We try to put off the fire from ever starting — that's preventive diplomacy. So I'm just emphasizing importance of preventive diplomacy and mediation and facilitation. This is far less expensive."

> Power of persuasion and dialogue with concerned parties. We try to focus on preventive diplomacy, mediation and facilitation. If we can mediate between the conflicting parties, we can prevent war.

"To catch it before it breaks out."

"Oh yes, yes."

"How do you do that? In speeches?"

"Yes, in speeches, but nobody pays attention, until fire actually breaks out. However much I say 'let us try to prevent this conflict', they don't pay attention. It is only when they see the fire, do they bring all their water hoses and try to put out the fire … and then people might say, oh, he [the UNSG] is very dynamic, such a strong leader … that's the general perception. So, of course, when there is no war, there is no hero."

That's a good line.

R2P

"Now we have a very important new concept about peace and, again, it is about protecting people from war and genocide. I have presented 'responsibility to protect' as a very important concept for the United Nations today. We call it R2P, responsibility to protect. This concept was adopted in 2005. Because we have seen the Rwanda genocide, and we have seen genocide in Srebrenica, Yugoslavia, and we have seen the Cambodia killing fields … then how to prevent mass murder, mass atrocities and genocide, crimes against humanity and ethnic cleansing and war crimes? Those are major, major crimes that must be abolished in the name of humanity.

"But then nothing had been implemented, so when I was campaigning for this office [in 2006], I said publicly that if elected, I will put this concept of responsibility-to-protect into action. But there was strong resistance from member states. Even though leaders agreed to the concept, the problem was in implementing, in translating, this into action. [There was] a lot of resistance. Gradually and persistently I have been trying to expand the level of understanding, and I have appointed a special advisor for that."

"Special advisor for what?"

"Now, this is very interesting. I wanted to appoint a special advisor on R2P, and they said no, they didn't agree."

"Who? Security Council?"

"No, many member states, particularly from the Third World, developing countries. Then finally I just appointed a special advisor."

"Period. No R2P title."

"With understanding that he will do—"

"R2P!"

"R2P! I appointed him for only $1 a year, a one-dollar-a-year job, it's pro bono, all pro bono."

"You're going to pay the $1 out of your pocket?"

"Yes, $1! He's on his own cost. Only then I was able to have somebody for the office. Last year we finally brought this to the General Assembly. So they discussed it more, but they are no more fully open to embracing this one."

"Is it for the obvious reason that a strong R2P office might threaten their ability to run their countries with total, if not criminal, autonomy?"

He nods: "But we don't want to repeat any Rwanda genocide. So, of course, in a case when a country is not able to control the situation, where it may develop into genocide, ethnic cleansing, war crimes, crimes against humanity, then should we just sit and watch under the pretext, the principle, of sovereignty? So one country may say, 'Well, this is our internal matter. We have a sovereign right and you should not come in.' This is our concept, but people are not wholeheartedly open to it. While many developed countries support this, there are still many developing countries that do not."

"Where does one of your great supporters, China, stand on R2P?"

"China is in the middle. They say ok. They don't publicly oppose."

Me asking: "But as you know, they have this doctrine of non-interference in the internal affairs of states, so under that doctrine, the UN had better not be interfering in the internal affairs of states on a preemptive basis."

The truth is that the U.S. and China are closer together on this basic issue than perhaps either would care to

> I have presented 'responsibility to protect' as a very important concept for the United Nations today. We call it R2P ... This concept was adopted in 2005... how to prevent mass murder, mass atrocities and genocide, crimes against humanity and ethnic cleansing and war crimes? Those are major, major crimes that must be abolished in the name of humanity.

admit. Beijing doesn't want the UN telling it how to comport itself in the seas around it, and the U.S. is hostile to the idea that its forays into other countries (invasion of Iraq, drone drilling into Pakistan) should require UN Security Council authorization. And neither of them is a big fan of the UNSG being equipped with an always-ready-to-go standing army.

"That's what many developing countries worry [about especially]. They worry that big countries, Western powers, in the name of humanity, may just come into their country and take charge. This is an unsubstantiated concern, so I'm in the process of convincing them to please don't worry, we have four distinct, clear benchmarks. These are crimes against humanity, genocide, ethnic cleansing and war crimes."

For example, he notes: "Now, Bashir, President Bashir of Sudan, was charged for crimes against humanity last year; he was charged again for genocide."

In 2010 President Bashir was charged by the International Criminal Court. And thus began a domino effect of crumbling autocratic regimes — the so-called Arab Spring.

In 2011, under UN supervision, and with the personal involvement of the SG, the southern part of Sudan was broken off and became the new nation of South Sudan. The intention was to separate the warring tribes and factions with a new national boundary. South Sudan became the 193rd member state of the UN. By the first half of 2012, less than a year later, the two started going at it again, this time as warring states.

So it goes. It's a Hobbesian world.

BEYOND NATIONAL INTEREST

Ban explains: "This is why I have to be above national interests. I have to take care of global issues. So my message to national leaders, and particularly the young generation, has always been widen your scope, and look beyond your national boundaries and try to become a global citizen. That is the best way for everyone to contribute."

He is almost philosophical now — a workingman's disciple of the American philosopher Martha Nussbaum. It was this smart lady who has so well articulated a far-reaching vision of cosmopolitanism — that everyone on this planet should give our allegiance to no mere national government, no temporal power, but to the moral community made up of the humanity of all human beings.

He nods and recalls one of the most memorable moments of his life when he met a living example of political cosmopolitanism: "One person who much impressed me was Nelson Mandela. I met him as secretary general and was particularly moved when I thanked him and I expressed my respect for what he did to contribute to humanity by enduring all these hardships and by getting the apartheid policy abolished. His reply was, 'No, it's not only me, there are hundreds of thousands, known and unknown, who contributed.' I thought at first he was just saying this out of a humble way, but then we were continuing our dialogue. I again expressed my thanks and his answer was the same, 'No, it was not only me, there are hundreds and thousands of people, known and unknown…' He repeated 'known and unknown people' again and again, he said they are the real contributors."

"The known and the unknown … it's a good phrase, isn't it?"

"That really shocked me … how? He's a great man!"

Imagine, if instead of breeding body-wielding suicide bomb terrorists, we started breeding more 'positive sleeper-selves'! I try this as a play on the nasty kind of 'sleeper-cells'.

He likes it: "Oh yes!"

"Positive-sleeper-selves that can be triggered if you say the right thing … like when a Mandela says the right thing."

"I've been repeating, conveying this to my staff, my meeting with Nelson Mandela."

Ban claims that to observe Mandela is almost to receive a vision of what a person of genuine nobility ought to be like, so as to be able to rise above the dreary everyday swirl of life. Take the rough battleground of the UN Secretariat, where bad, as well as good, things happen every day: "It always comes back to me, and I don't avoid my responsibility. People, when they criticize organizations, then it's always the secretary general … so then I don't duck it."

UN STAFF

There is good news as well as bad in the composition of the sizable staff of international civil servants at headquarters in New York.

Ban: "The strength of UN staff is that they provide diverse experience and perspectives. The weakness is the fuzzy chains of command. This place is a huge, multilateral organization composed of all different nationalities. Sometimes it's apt to lose focus. So unless I become disciplined and try to be very clear, it's very difficult to understand what is going on down there, for as a matter of principle I give almost full independence to the under secretaries general of the departments. There are many departments and the head of each department is topped by an under secretary general or an assistant secretary general. Though they are the senior staff, nobody enjoys full independence; when it comes to sensitive and important decisions, they have to bring [it up to the secretary general] with some options. And these options are discussed fully and then I finally make my choice — and sometimes it's a very difficult decision. It's not like decisions made by national leaders. It's the UN. You have to review all the complex views of stakeholders and interested parties. It's not so unitary, it's not one line of command."

Everyone makes mistakes, and when they happen, Ban feels he needs to light a candle at the altar of St. Mandela and realize that his life was so much more difficult and painful than his own. So let's try to contain the temper tantrums and take it all in stride.

Me asking: "So if there is a mistake, you may say privately to your staff that 'you screwed up on that one', but you will take the heat. Is that right? Are you thinking of yourself as some sort of saint or what?"

"No," he says, laughing, "I'm not a saint. I always tell my staff that when I recruit senior advisors. I place emphasis on teamwork. Even though one may come with less experience, even at a less intellectual level, I would rather have somebody who is a person of teamwork, working as a team player. I've been telling my staff that I would not blame anybody who would make a small or a big mistake — if they are working hard and doing their best as a team member. But I would be angry and really critical if somebody makes mistakes just to avoid responsibility, not doing enough.

"By doing that I'm giving full power, full confidence, to the people, no matter whether in the course of delivering results, one may make certain misjudgments or mistakes … that's not important. That normally happens in any society, in any organization. In such a case, I take all political responsibility. So I made it quite clear to my staff — I will take all political responsibility, whatever comes to me."

> I take all political responsibility. I made it clear to my staff — I will take all political responsibility, whatever comes to me.

Me saying: "Now when you do that, do you do that first of all because you're a man of honor? The Confucian gentleman? But it is also a clever management tool, right? Say someone works with you and he or she screws up, of course didn't mean to screw up, but did. Then, instead of your saying, yes we did have a mistake and it was all Plate's fault, you would rather take the heat. Then the staffer feels like my boss really is a standup guy so now I'm going to work even harder and not screw up the next time. Is that in the back of your mind, or is it just the honor thing? Isn't it a management tool as well?"

Ban is nodding enthusiastically: "That's right. When I was a junior officer, I used to tell my friends and colleagues that whoever really honors me and trusts me, then I would do whatever ... I would go till the ends of this earth, but whatever is not honorable, whatever is against my principles, then I would not obey any such order or instruction."

"If you were in Nazi Germany, you would not have—"

"In effect that's what I'm saying to many national leaders who are rightly being criticized for violation of human rights, certain principles that are universally accepted."

NATURAL EVOLUTION OF HISTORY

"You have had some lively conversations with President Assad of Syria. How would a conversation with Assad go? I mean, you pick up the phone and you call him, or he calls you, when he is probably shooting people?"

"Oh, yes. Of course."

"What do you say to him? How do you say it?"

"First, I express my deepest concerns on the ongoing situation where people are being killed, so I urge him to stop 'killing your own people'. Killing your own people is a dead-end, and this is a violation of International human rights law and international humanitarian law. You should listen attentively, and seriously, to the challenges and aspirations of your people ... what your people are asking you to do. Please engage in inclusive dialogue, and make bold and decisive reform before it is too late."

Ban peers out towards the river-view window. The horrid weather hasn't let up.

"All those are points which I have been speaking [about] to Assad. Not only Assad but to Gaddafi and to many other leaders of the region, in Bahrain and in Yemen ... all these areas. And I have been talking to many other leaders. Even where there were not demonstrations but there were some symptoms, which we recognized, I would call the leaders of those countries [and ask them] to start bold political reform. And many countries in their region have announced political reform, constitutional amendments. I think that's a good, positive thing. I believe that what we have witnessed in that region is a natural evolution of history."

"Natural evolution of history?"

"This is a once-in-a-generation opportunity. We have seen such demonstrations and struggles for democracy in the 1950s. In Hungary, in 1956, of course, they were oppressed then by the Soviet Union. We have seen it in Korea, 1960 until late 1980s, where people and students went to the streets and started calling for democratic reforms, greater freedom and greater participatory democracy. [South] Korea has been able to achieve full democracy. We have seen in the late 80s the downfall of communism, the disintegration of the Soviet Union and the birth of new Eastern European countries, where we have seen all their struggling, the yearning for freedom and democracy."

Ban is clearly moved: "Now, only after that, we are seeing this Arab Spring in the Arab world. People have been oppressed in the name of this tradition or that, or because of religious belief, or by long-standing, long-serving monarchical systems. In particular, women's rights have been totally neglected in those parts of the world. Now is the right time for change, and we are witnessing this history. That is why I have been urging people around the world to be part of this. Let us not be just bystanders. Let us be a part of this."

> Killing your own people is a dead-end ... You should listen attentively, and seriously, to ... what your people are asking you to do. Please engage in inclusive dialogue, and make bold and decisive reform before it is too late.

"A part of history."

"Part of history. And let us feel pride when all these people in the region are able to enjoy their democracy and freedom. Then, after 10 years, or 20 years, I will be explaining things to my grandchildren, and you will be telling your children and grandchildren, look, I was part of this, I witnessed this myself, and I feel proud that people are now enjoying genuine freedom and democracy. I've been urging them: Let us be part of this. Let us be part of these historic, evolutionary changes."

Ban watched his breath, then continued: "Look at what has happened in Libya, and also the situation in Syria."

It's hard to imagine Ban's patience doing much to soften the stubborn Syrian dictator. "How many conversations do you think you had with Assad?"

"Assad? Since the beginning of this current crisis, five times. But we have this indirect dialogue through [special envoy] Kofi Annan. But before that, I had a lot of conversations with him. At first my relationship with Assad was, I think, rather cordial and friendly."

"Uh-huh, at first…"

He nods: "At first, and I really wanted to help him — to bring Syria into open society, to help Assad find his rightful place. He was totally isolated even before this crisis, in the Arab world, not to mention among the Western powers."

"But he's a tough customer, isn't he?"

"Tough customer, yes." Ban shakes his head gravely.

It's sort of ghoulish, with so many people dying in Syria, but I have to laugh.

Ban continuing: "Now, I'm not a psychologist, I'm not able to fathom what mental psychological situation he is in, but as a human being he must be terribly crazy or insane, out of his mind. He has gone too far, too deep, it's too late for him now to return to normalcy.

"Even now, what he has to do is, before it's too late, he has to decide on his own future as well as on his country's future. If he still thinks he's a leader of his country, if he still thinks *that* after leading his country over 10 years, then he should know what to do for his own country and his own people. But I'm afraid that he's not able to make his own decision, being surrounded by all those hardliners who believe that if Assad falls, they will fall … and Assad may believe that if they do not support him he may fall. So he must be psychologically terribly isolated and terrified. That's one thing I'm very much afraid [about], especially when we are pushing for a diplomatic and political solution."

"But Assad's not going to step down, right?"

"That's a problem. But we discussed the possible deployment of observers to make sure that both sides will stop and will not engage further in violent fighting. But that should be preceded by an Assad unilateral ceasefire which will have to be supported by opposition forces."

Ban refers to his experience with the crisis in Gaza, the one in January 2008. Instead of trying to put together a complex simultaneous ceasefire, Ban sometimes recommends starting with a unilateral approach that can put pressure on the other parties to follow suit. Think of the procedure, he suggests, as setting up a kind of serial ceasefire system.

> At first my relationship with Assad was, I think, rather cordial and friendly … and I really wanted to help him — to bring Syria into open society, to help Assad find his rightful place. He was totally isolated, even before this crisis, in the Arab world, not to mention among the Western powers.

"During that time I had been traveling in the region meeting with the leaders, President Abbas and, most importantly, Prime Minister Olmert of Israel. All the leaders at that time were trying to put together our ceasefire, like President Sarkozy, but they all failed because they were all working for a simultaneous ceasefire between Israelis and Hamas.

"I was also trying for that, but following round after round of meetings with leaders, I found out that it would be impossible. The only way would be a unilateral ceasefire by Olmert, because the Israelis started this war and they should stop. I met Olmert, I think three times, made a lot of telephone calls to him, and finally, he agreed. Then I went to Lebanon. During that night Olmert issued an order for a unilateral ceasefire.

"After that, I said Hamas should do the same, must cooperate by agreeing to a ceasefire. So the next morning, I flew immediately to Damascus, for just a very brief visit. I had a one-hour talk with President Assad. It was, I think, my second time meeting with him. I had been speaking over the phone with him many times on that ceasefire issue, and then I flew to Damascus and convinced him that you have a role to play now, why don't you talk to the Hamas people who are accommodated in Damascus. His name is Khaled Mashaal, the head of Hamas. He told me, well, I'll do my best. From there, I flew to Egypt where President Obama, President Sarkozy, Angela Merkel of Germany, Zapatero of Spain, the King of Jordan and all these leaders were gathered. While there, I received a note from the Syrian ambassador saying that Hamas, upon Assad's influence, will announce a ceasefire. It was done, it was done!

"So it took less than 12 hours since the announcement by Prime Minister Olmert of Israel for unilateral ceasefire. Hamas agreed, so that's why Gaza peace is now the reality, even though occasional sporadic violence still takes place. There is a ceasefire, not a permanent ceasefire, but it's still working — that's the point I raised.

"In Syria they are fighting in a disproportionate way. Assad has a very strong, regular national army. These are disorganized opposition forces, as President Obama put it — ragtag, ragtag. I discussed this matter with the president. He agreed to my idea that, while these are all disorganized ragtag forces, we have to influence them to agree to the ceasefire. So, you see, once Assad makes a unilateral decision, things happen. So this is our approach now though, unfortunately, we have not been able to get that.

"If and when, after our conversation, Assad does agree, I think it will be in that form."

But the UN effort to get Assad to agree could well fail. If it did, wouldn't it be regarded as Ban's fault, I ask.

Ban feels he has done more to take on these national bullies than people realize.

"Many people were surprised when I spoke out — have we seen any such in secretaries general? It was me who had spoken out for the first time, for the first time, asking [former Egyptian president] Hosni Mubarak to go. I said, 'Now — he must go.'"

"And in Libya! In fact, you were so out in front in Libya that you were asked by some in other states not to be so far ahead. Didn't Washington at one point say you were too far out front?"

He nods. He doesn't really want to get into this but at some point, he feels, fair is only fair: "Yeah, I know. It took nine days — *nine* days! — for President Obama to come out and say something about Libya, you know, about Gaddafi. But I was the first leader to speak out."

GOLDEN PARACHUTE FOR TYRANTS?

I say it's hard to see what's irrational about the desire of the extreme autocrat to hang on to power, from his point of view.

Me pointing out: "Just look what's happened to everyone who's stepped down. Mubarak's in jail, Saddam Hussein went into a hole and then was executed. I mean, unless you can offer Assad a position at Harvard Law School — which as a method of law student ethics improvement could create something of a moral hazard, there's a problem — right?"

"Yeah, I have something to say about that."

Let's press the point then: "Do you think that, if the world would accept a kind of moral blindness — which is to say, bribing bad guys with a good retirement package — but suppose a good retirement package would get a Sudanese Bashir out, or a Syrian Bashar Assad…"

"That's a very interesting question."

"Right. You see what I'm saying?"

Ban does indeed: "When I was meeting many leaders in the region, Africa and Arab, Middle East, they were saying, in a similar way, if you're indicted by the International Criminal Court, and if they lift their hands [to give up], then they'll be arrested and pursued by ICC. So then Assad sees he has no future … he has gone too far, too deep. There's no way for him to find any exit. If he retires, if he steps down, then there will be ICC prosecutions or some other revolutionary counter-measures. Then there's only one way for him to stick to his power."

Is there no out-of-the-box, even way out idea?

Consider the philosophy of Mohammed Ibrahim, the founder of a mobile phone company in Africa and the Middle East that was fabulously successful (like Thaksin's in Asia in the 1990s). His foundation used some of those huge gains to fund a retirement program for African heads of state who leave their country better off than when they went in, rather than take out all the gains and park them in secret accounts. At this writing, three very substantial awards have been given.

So here is a thought: Why not set up a foundation for ultra nasty dictators? For those who should be ousted but so fear ICC persecution, poverty and death that they respond with brutal revenge attacks to all challengers to their over-staying rule?

For obvious reasons, the SG can't say it, but why don't we? In some cases it might save countless lives to buy out a dictator rather than to try to shoot our way in. Immoral? Not if many thousands of lives are saved! Amoral, perhaps, but well worth considering. Lives are always worth saving. Indeed, it might be considered quite moral to do so.

THE MOST PART OF ALL PRINCES HAVE
MORE DELIGHT IN WARLIKE MANNERS
AND FEATS OF CHIVALRY THAN IN
GOOD FEATS OF PEACE.

– Utopia

Women and Ban

Looking down at their shoes ...
not a utopian world ... isn't it a pity?

LIKE ME, YOU might have thought it strange, too, when the secretary general of the United Nations unabashedly revealed that a favorite movie is *G.I. Jane*. This was the 1997 U.S. action movie directed by Ridley Scott. A classic like *All Quiet on the Western Front* — or for that matter *The Iron Lady* — it was not.

The unexpected film review occurs at a Manhattan venue known for especially talented performers. The late singer Bobby Short used to hold forth nightly at Café Carlyle in the Carlyle Hotel; on Monday nights, the director and writer Woody Allen jauntily toots his clarinet with his New Orleans Jazz Band. And on this Friday night, the café's compact stage features Bettye LaVette, the R&B soul singer.

Aside from diplomatic obligations, Soon-taek and Ki-moon rarely get out to occupy the smothering UN embrace of meetings, receptions and official occasions. This is where I self-appointed myself to help out. On every trip to New York for our conversations, I would propose one night out after one of our two-hour conversations, for dinner and/or maybe a show. The Bans could say yes, or they could say no. My memory tells me they never did say no, actually.

Tonight it was both a dinner and the LaVette show. The 65-year-old performer was well known for her struggle to escape the poverty of Detroit and realize her dream as a premier entertainer. Her struggle was successful, propelled by talent and drive. So she seemed like a good bet for the Bans, especially for Soon-taek, with her near-encyclopedic appreciation of stage theater and music, but also for her husband, who has made more than a little of his empathy for women's-rights struggles.

But his thumbs-up for *G.I. Jane* — that caught me totally off guard! Starring Demi Moore, the movie was a cartoonish feminist film depicting the struggles of the first woman to be admitted to the famous — if (by the film's depiction) notoriously punishing and sexist — Navy Seals training program.

Ban would be the first to concede he was no film buff like his wife. Over the decades as a workaholic career diplomat, he didn't have time for that, after all. But something in the cartoon-like movie deeply moved Ki-moon (and he was to meet Ms. Moore at a symposium in Los Angeles on how Hollywood could enhance the UN's image). As the waiter began placing salads on the tiny table allegedly for four, Ban admitted he practically stood up and roared when Moore — a.k.a. G.I. Jane — completed the near-impossible training and became a bona-fide Seal.

Ban has spent 40 years with the same woman — a Korean woman, of course — born and bred in the Confucian Korean value-system of the traditional family and hierarchical social structure.

Waiters bustling about — but, seemingly, almost no one in the café noticing or caring that the UN chief is here — he turns to me and mentions that Robert Orr, a well regarded senior UN official who is American (via UCLA, Princeton and Harvard), has a Korean wife too.

Me laughing: "Oh, is that right? So the successful American diplomats at the UN, they have to have good Korean wives!"

Soon-taek is chatting with Andrea, but the café noise is so loud that the ladies on other side of the tiny table are into their own conversation that we boys cannot hear — sort of like North and South Korea.

Ban turns to me and laughs and jabs back: "In fact, I have another top aide, one very good able spokesperson who is British … he also has a Korean wife."

I think I see a pattern here.

He says jokingly: "I didn't check that they had Korean wives before I hired them."

"Sure you did! That's why they got the job! The Korean Wives' Club."

In fact, at the beginning of 2007, as Ban was quite warily entering the Secretariat, he brought along a retinue of male Koreans — almost like trailing spouses, as it were — to man his core palace guard. They were to serve him as Korean mandarins, and serve him well indeed, perhaps too well. In the process of protecting him, they quickly morphed into tempting targets for those smooth-as-silk UN Secretariat traditionalists whose favorite retort to the newbie Korean Guard was a dismissive, "We don't do things that way at the UN" or … "those f---ing Koreans that surround him."

That brittle and sometimes bruising battle of egos may for a time have diverted the Secretariat from getting the full view of the real Ban. It turns out that this Korean gentleman in his sixties is practically obsessed with women's rights, and for reasons that relate to his relationship not only with his mother but his wife.

Ban has this to say about Korean women today: "Yes, I have seen so many able and passionate women in Korea. Often there is a tendency to believe that South Korean women are very shy, obedient, faithful and calm. But socially they have become quite active and most of the Korean names known internationally were or have been women. You try to find any Korean man's name that's prominent these days, not easy…"

He's right when you think about it.

"…whose names have been internationally recognized, I think maybe just one or two, like President Kim Dae-jung or myself. Even Korean presidents, their names are not internationally recognized. But you will see lots of Korean women's names when it comes to golf, skating, different sports … women. We have only one man whose name is recognized in world sports now, in golf. Korean women are very active socially, and I believe in the power and capacity of women."

LOOKING DOWN AT THEIR SHOES

One member of LaVette's band hops on stage to start the setup. We have both now turned our backs on our wives to face the action. We can't hear them anyway.

"But I thought South Korea was a male-dominated society that kept women at home, pregnant and Confucian-submissive."

Ban's voice is spotty again from the day's speechmaking: "Yes, everybody believes that South Korea is a macho, male-dominated society, but behind this scene it's women who really dominate and control the family life and a lot of other things."

The thin drummer looks as pale as a ghost in serious pain.

"On the cutting edge of modernizing South Korean women, besides golfers and ice skaters and professors, are there any Korean diplomats who are women?"

"We have a lot of women Korean diplomats now, they are coming up. Now more than 50 percent new recruits are women."

"In the Korean foreign service?" It's not generally known but the professionals in the Republic of Korea's foreign affairs ministry are well regarded internationally.

"Yes, yes. There used be very few. At one time there were no women diplomats and I was the first foreign minister who appointed two women ambassadors, career ambassadors and even directors general. I was the first one to try to promote women. Progress on this issue depends upon political will ...political will."

He stares at you through those medicinal-looking bifocals as if he means business. I still feel I am missing something. Is this strong feeling about women's justice but an agenda thing?

I try it this way: "Do the ambitious Korean women you tend to meet regard the efforts of American women here as something that has benefited them? I mean, do they admire the American feminist movement for showing them the way?"

"I think this feminist group's advocacy for women's rights has clearly helped. That was the inspiration to change the dynamics and beliefs among political leaders."

But what is really behind this? Just smart-eyed international politics? After all, the fact is that with Hillary Clinton, the U.S. fronted a woman secretary of state, and so did the Bush administration with Rice. Germany's Angela Merkel is probably Europe's best leader. Politically volatile Thailand finally has a woman prime minister. But Korea has never sported a significant female political leader. Perhaps he feels guilty about that; surely he feels guilty about something.

He looks downward and says: "Of course there are changes in Korea. As you say, people may speak correct things but deeds may not match their words. But I might have a different feeling because I was raised under such circumstances. And I was influenced by my wife, who would often say, 'Look, why do men have such narrow minds? After all, it's a male's world. When you see a few women rising, why are you men so jealous and critical about women? After all, you have been dominating this world for thousands of years, since the beginning of mankind. And now women are coming up. Then why are you men so narrow-minded to not encourage them?'

That struck me so much, so as soon as I became secretary general, I checked on the status of women in power here. There were few women senior advisors. When I say senior advisors, I mean at the under secretary general level. The highest-level appointment I can make is under secretary general."

The thin drummer gives the rim of the snare drum a few quick shots.

Ban takes a sip of red wine and continues: "For example, when I appointed the former president of Chile, Michelle Bachelet, she went to the level of under secretary general. I was able to establish this super UN women's agency that she headed. But it took four years!"

> ...as soon as I became secretary general, I checked on the status of women in power here. There were few women senior advisors.

Also especially notable was Ban's special effort to secure a top UN appointment for the very competent Helen Clark, former prime minister of New Zealand. Ban recounts these appointments as a battle against the status quo.

The drummer waves to the piano player who has hopped up onto the other side of the stage with a raft of sheet music.

Ban saying: "Sure, it's encouraging that in the 21st century, women's role and status are being recognized, but to continue that, you need to have political leaders' commitment. It will take a long time to change deeply rooted traditions, so unless you establish a very firm policy priority in all institutions, further change will be difficult. That's what I did in the United Nations. When I became secretary general, there were just a few women in important positions, very few senior women advisors at the rank of under secretary general. In my first three years, by giving the issue political priority, I changed the whole situation, increased by 60 percent those women senior advisors at the rank of under secretary general. Above the rank of assistant secretary general, it is 40 percent increased. It's not 40 persons but a 40-percent increase — this is unprecedented. Then, I have changed the positions which have been occupied solely by men during the last 65 years with women … many such positions."

> In my first three years, by giving the issue political priority, I changed the whole situation, increased by 60 percent those women senior advisors at the rank of under secretary general. Above the rank of assistant secretary general, it is 40 percent increased. It's not 40 persons but a 40-percent increase — this is unprecedented.

He shakes his head and looks at me as if it took the Second Korean War to get all this done: "At first some UN people found this very strange and were reluctant to recognize this kind of drastic change. Sometimes when a senior position was open, all the names presented to me as candidates were men, just 1-2-3, men. So I asked them to provide me with more choices, but the tradition was 1-2-3 all men, as my predecessors used to decide among men, so there was no chance for women."

I look over my shoulder and Soon-taek and Andrea are still talking, probably about movies. Mrs. Ban loves them and Andrea has been in a few of them, as the child actress Andrea Darvi, long ago.

"So I thought that by accepting that selection process, I would never be able to change anything ... and of course the selection committee was full of men. So, first of all, I changed the composition of the committee so that it should be equally balanced, and said that when there were three names submitted, there had to be one woman's name, at least one. Then when I was given three names, without any women, I would just return all these names, and by doing that I was eventually able to find a senior woman to appoint."

His media-relations people had already laid out these facts, which are in fact true. So I say: "I know what you're saying is fact-based, but what I'm trying to get at is, even if Hillary Clinton were not secretary of state of the United States, you would have done this, I think."

He looks at me with a little distaste. "Yes."

But it is politically correct — as well as an absolute matter of justice and fairness — to champion women's causes. Indeed, in America, the foolish man who doesn't can put his life, or at least his career, at risk! Yet for Korean men of Ban's generation, it's not always the case that women's rights occupy the top of their list of priorities and preoccupations.

But Ban is different. Something else is going on.

So I say: "All the Korean males that I have met, of your generation, have traditional attitudes toward women. The men want the women to be in the home, but when one brings up women's issues, you know, they say the right things, even if their true beliefs are elsewhere. But there's probably one singular exception to that, and honestly, that's you. I've thought about it and so I have to wonder. Why Ban Ki-moon?"

An aide had told me the key to finding Ban's core on the women's issue was probably to do with the experience of his mother, at this writing 91 years old, living back in South Korea.

"Let's go back to your youth in war-ravaged Korea. Poor women who were pregnant literally risked their lives giving birth, right? Health conditions were so bad then?"

The secretary general nodded as if he understood the implications of the question. Maybe the aide had tipped him off that I would ask this.

"That's what my mother told me when I was young. In Korea then, there was hardly any sanitary or health support for anybody, including women. So a most difficult time for women was to give birth. There weren't even midwives, only experienced women in the village. They would come to help another pregnant woman to deliver. It was always dangerous. So the Korean women, I was told by my mother, they would always stop and stare before going into a certain room for giving birth. They would stare down at their rubber shoes.

"You see, at the time, Korean women were wearing shoes of

only very simple primitive rubber. So the woman would wonder whether, after giving birth, she would live to be able to wear those shoes again. This might be the last time, if she would not be successful ... if anything goes wrong."

"To never wear and walk in those rubber shoes again, you mean? If they didn't get to live through the ordeal of the day of giving birth?"

"Yes, yes. That really hit my heart."

NOT A UTOPIAN WORLD

This was the world of the Korean Peninsula in the war-torn 50s. It was an anti-utopian world — life tended toward the nasty, brutish and sometimes short. It's difficult for Koreans from that era, now at least in their sixties, to imagine being anti-American unless they are comfortable imagining a peninsula united under communism. But just one glance north in the direction of the disaster that is the "Democratic People's Republic of Korea" undermines that frivolous thought.

You can almost feel the UN secretary general shudder as he recalls that time: "In fact, on the third day of the Korean War, my mother [Shin Hyun-soon] had to flee from the shelling and fighting with my sister who was born while we were escaping to another village."

Hyun-soon was in her late twenties. "Just steps ahead of the invading army, fleeing as fast as her ill-fitting rubber shoes would permit, the newborn in her arms?"

Ban nods: "Yes, when the Chinese invaded in 1951 and my mother gave birth to my sister ... it was a very cold January. She had to walk and flee with the newly born child, just a three-day-old child. Since then my mother's health has never been good because of the after-effect of that childbirth long ago."

He recaptures his UNSG official voice after almost cracking: "Today, the UN regards the maternal health and newborn child health issue as one of the most serious. Every single minute, one woman dies [unnecessarily]; so while we are talking in this comfortable way, in the next two hours an average of 120 women will have died during this time. This is morally unacceptable."

Ban speaks with deep conviction. In the course of my career, perhaps no Korean male of his generation has seemed more sincere on this matter than Ki-moon, at least to me.

"Of course, in South Korea now, it is much better with modern health systems and facilities, but there are many countries where just being admitted to hospital is a privilege. There are so many people who are dying without being able to even go near a medical facility. That's a fact of life at this time. So maternal and child health issues are going to be most important. How to reduce the mortality rate, maternal mortality rate and child mortality rate — this is one of the top concerns."

I have to go back to his mother's moving story: "Do you remember when your mother first told you about women who 'look down at their shoes'?"

"Oh, when I was a very young boy. I was in middle school ...

early 1960s."

"I don't want to get into amateur psychiatry, but that is one of your mother's stories you really remember the most?"

"That's right … that's right."

"It is very sad. Imagine you're waiting to go in the room to give birth and you're looking down at your shoes and you're wondering if you'll ever wear them again, because once you are dead, someone else will get them."

"Oh yes. That's real. And it's why this maternal health issue is part of gender equality. Why are they not given enough support? But in actual life, for many centuries, women have been just disregarded and ignored in our society. That was the case in South Korea too, as in most Asian countries. Even in the Western countries, women's political status was recognized very late."

Me pressing on: "So there are three big reasons prompting your views on women. One is that it's just the right thing to do; two, the inspirational examples of ambitious, successful, up-and-coming Korean women; and, three, your mom looking down at her shoes. Is that it?"

"Yes, that's right."

"Because you do have a special feel on this."

The second half of the backup quartet arrives. The show at the Café Carlyle is about to start.

Ban saying: "What I mean is, there needs to be a political system which will support this change, otherwise change may depend entirely upon a leader. My philosophy is that you need to have a system that sustains this momentum in the future. Now, for the first time in 65 years of UN history, we have established an unprecedented super women's agency just dealing with women."

Adopted by the General Assembly, its formal institutional title is UN WOMEN: United Nations Entity for Gender Equality and the Empowerment of Women.

"I have been working very hard, much differently from my predecessors, on gender equality, women's empowerment. It's revolutionary in a sense that I have changed many men-leaders to women-leaders. It was quite difficult. There were a lot [of people] in opposition from the 'male world'. This is, after all, a male-dominated society. The United Nations is no exception. You would be surprised. Now it has been recognized by many people around the world that I changed it a lot. Not only have I spoken, as a matter of principle, I have led by example."

ISN'T IT A PITY?
He clears his throat again: "But there was a lot of opposition."

"Member states?"

"Member states. And even in the women's community, there were some controversies. They were not willing to get integrated into one big agency. It was very difficult. There used to be four different departments or agencies, but we integrated all into this one, and this took four years."

I then ask: "Would you welcome your successor being a woman?"

"Yes, I would. There was a strong wish from the women's community when I was running for this, and it is high time the world's women argued for a woman secretary general of the United Nations."

That's not a bad idea.

"I thought that maybe the least utilized resource in the world is women's full capacities. We have explored all this gas, oil, all these natural resources [laughing] but we cannot properly utilize women? My wife has been telling me all the time that if women got control of society, there'd be less war, less conflict."

"Do you believe that?"

> I have been working very hard, much differently from my predecessors, on gender equality, women's empowerment. It's revolutionary in a sense that I have changed many men-leaders to women-leaders ... Now it has been recognized by many people ... that I changed it a lot. Not only have I spoken, as a matter of principle, I have led by example.

"I do. Men become so narrow minded. 'Why don't you become magnanimous and broad-minded,' my wife used to tell me."

"Well, you speak very passionately, and I'm glad that you listened carefully to Mrs. Ban, because she has wisdom."

"She's a great, soft person, and she doesn't speak out much, but sometimes when she speaks…"

"When your wife speaks to you on this issue, she has great influence and you really listen. One reason you listen is because in

> ❝ I thought that maybe the least utilized resource in the world is women's full capacities. We have explored all this gas, oil, all these natural resources … but we cannot properly utilize women? ❞

a way, she gave up her career in library science all for you."

"Oh yes! Yes."

I push this point: "Not just a library job but all of it. You know, maybe she could be head of Seoul National University Library today or something like that, or whatever a top-level librarian position would be. But she gave all that up to be your wife, to bear your children, to take care of the grandchildren, while you go around the world being a superstar. And she gave all that up, she gave up her professional career, for you."

"That's true. That's right, I'm grateful to her."

"Grateful, sure! But isn't there a little guilt too? Just a little guilt?"

He pauses, looks over his shoulder at Soon-taek, and says: "Yes, guilt, too."

He looks downcast, a weight on his conscience.

Then he looks up at me with emotion in his eyes.

"You see, when we married, at that time in Korea, the fear was that there were not enough jobs to go around, even for men. When a woman marries, gets married, at that time [it was the custom that] they should give up this position for men. So she was advised to tender her resignation after we got married."

"I see, she was advised—"

"Yes, back then women were advised. I remember that she was crying, but there was no way for her."

"…to stay at work at the university library?"

"Yes, yes … Joong-ang University in Seoul."

"And she was told, now that you have a husband, now that you have a breadwinner, you should give this position up for a man, so you should quit? And that was the end of her career?"

He nods.

The lights dim and Bettye LaVette pops out from a door behind the bar and through the audience, and up on the stage. She is tall, athletic, lively and 65. She prances in her high heels, shakes her hips in a tight black dress, and moves the well-off audience from its complacency with unexpectedly sad renditions of otherwise settled classics.

Mrs. Ban gasps: "Oh, she is so thin!"

Somewhere into the second set, LaVette begins crooning a song about how she is getting old.

"That's me," Soon-taek says to us.

Maybe the song that hits Ban hardest is LaVette's deeply mournful "Isn't It a Pity!?" She sings the George Harrison lyrics slowly and even morosely:

Isn't it a pity
Isn't it a shame
How we break each other's hearts

And cause each other pain
How we take each other's love
Without thinking any more
Forgetting to give back
Isn't it a pity

I turn to Ban and suggest maybe LaVette could sing that to open the next session of the General Assembly and Security Council. He starts to laugh hard and his face opens into a million smiling cracks, but then he stops himself: Ban Ki-moon, always the diplomat.

WE DID NOT ASK IF HE HAD SEEN
ANY MONSTERS, FOR MONSTERS
HAVE CEASED TO BE NEWS. THERE IS
NEVER ANY SHORTAGE OF HORRIBLE
CREATURES WHO PREY ON HUMAN
BEINGS, SNATCH AWAY THEIR FOOD,
OR DEVOUR WHOLE POPULATIONS …

– Utopia

The Bosses of All Bosses

**The Fab Five … bit of Bolton … the beginning
of trouble… unjust to Japan … happy trickster …
step up, Korea and China**

On June 11, 2011, this is the way the Associated Press covered one of Ban's better days:

> "The UN General Assembly voted unanimously to give Ban Ki-moon a second term as secretary general, praising him for strengthening the role and visibility of the world body in difficult circumstances. The 192-member assembly gave the 67-year-old South Korean diplomat another five years at the helm of the UN by voice vote. He faced no opposition and was recommended by the Security Council for the new term, also by voice vote."

It is not common at UN headquarters in New York that they concur on something major easily and unanimously. So it is noteworthy that Ban's confirmation for a second term went without a hitch. Would that more vital issues surface on which concurrence is so quickly achieved!

The AP story also reflects well the reality about the way things work at the UN. The Security Council and the General Assembly rule the roost when they want to. It's possible for a secretary general to get around these twin towers of collective wisdom but it is not easy. I remind myself over and over of a precedent way back in history. It was designed to engineer an escape from the nothingness of the UN's basket of excessive checks and balances. It is called the 'Peking formula'. It drew for justification on little more than the general mandate of the UN to maintain international peace and security — and on the dashing risk-taking of then UN secretary general Dag Hammarskjold.

This makeshift ploy for the override of inaction first emerged unofficially during the Korean War. The Chinese had downed and imprisoned U.S. airmen. But the Security Council was mired in Cold War impasse. So Hammarskjold took it upon himself to fly to Beijing secretly to secure the airmen's release. The dramatic peace effort worked — and became a precedent option, though not often exercised.

But it was into just that pioneering pathway that Ban Ki-moon stepped when the Security Council was gridlocked over the Kosovo mess. In February 2008 the ethnic Albanian majority decided to declare independence from Serbia. Former UN peacekeeping official David Harland recalls that Ban, as well as many others, feared a "major re-escalation of the conflict [and] … launched an effort to 'manage down' the crisis. But with no instructions from a gridlocked Security Council, Ban may have stretched the authority of his office further than any of his predecessors since Dag Hammarskjold."

I am thinking of Kosovo as I walk over to the UNSG's home for another conversation. The UN secretary general is a vitally important player indeed. But the fact of the matter is that it is the UNSC and the UNGA that decide who will get to be the secretary general, as well as many other things ... when, of course, anything major gets decided at all. That, you see, is the rub. As the admiring Harland puts it: "Rather than being a model for future diplomatic activism, Ban's efforts in Kosovo possibly probed the outer limits of the authority of a UN secretary general."[2]

Frustration at, and indeed, within, the UN springs from the institution's penchant for indecisiveness. Most of the time the blame goes to the Security Council. And the heat for that often falls on the so-called "P-5". These are the "5-p"ermanent members of the Security Council.

Nothing serious or substantive, such as a resolution for imposing economic sanctions, dispatching a peacekeeping force or condemning a member state, can come out of the 15-member council, if any seven members get together and vote against it. Nine votes are needed for passage. So, logically, any combination of seven can kill a substantive resolution.

But *that* has not been the main problem.

It is the other way that absolutely nothing can get done that raises hackles. That is when the P-5 do not agree together — *all five*

2 See David Harland, "Kosovo and the UN," *Survival.* Vol. 52, No. 5. October–November 2010.

of them — on the issue before the council.

The UN Charter, which came into being in 1945, does not actually state that each of the permanent members gets the "veto power". But that is the way the media puts it when one or more of the five big ones — China, France, Great Britain, Russia, the United States — vote against a resolution.

Technically it's not a veto so much as the UN Charter requiring major-power unity for a substantive matter to pass. So even if only one of the big five falls out, the deal falls through completely. So, right, it's sort of a veto.

The idea didn't originate with Stalin, but the Soviet dictator was the most adamant for its incorporation. World War II was over, and winners ruled! And perhaps an argument, though a weak one, could be made that even today the P-5 deal has logic. The big five, after all, do include today's pinnacle pair — the United States of America, still the world's sole military superpower, and China, the world's most populous country.

But … France, Great Britain and … Russia?

Give us a break, complain India or Brazil or Germany, among others, not to mention economic giant Japan: What are we — some kind of South Sudan? (This is the 8-million-population mini-state broken off in 2011 from the oppressive Sudan, to become the 193rd UN member state.) Or Nauru (with a population of less than 10,000, a South Pacific island a few kilometers wide at most)? In the General Assembly, yes, these countries have the same vote as China or the U.S.

The claim then is that at the very structural heart of the UN throbs a living, functioning, continuing … artery of injustice — the Security Council. Five countries have the power to squeeze the life out of the entire UN, even if only one of the five has its nose out of joint. And so, as with all injustices, especially at the UN, people want to 'reform' the Security Council.

Walking along 57th Street amid the relative calm of a Saturday morning in Manhattan helps to sort out the issue.

Yes, it would be better if the Council were not so weighed down by the past that its future as a credible organization would be put in doubt time and again. Harland has summed it up nicely: "Ban's Kosovo maneuver may not be the shape of things to come for the UN, but, in the constrained world of multilateral diplomacy, it was a welcome return to Peking."

Yes, it would be nice indeed if France and Great Britain, as elegant European entities eager to see the UN excel, were to bow out as permanent members and make way for new blood in Asia and Latin America. But for Russia to be so gracious! *Please!*

But it is not going to happen. Or it's going to happen the day after all human greed vanishes … every single person stops lying … all rich people give away any ill-gotten gains … water is found on the moon… Santa Claus comes to town and stays until Easter to hook up with the Easter Bunny … *UTOPIA!*

Yet I wonder whether Ban is as cynical — or, to put it perhaps less cynically, realistic — about the prospect of UN Security Council reform. Why would any member of the permanent five actually vote for a reform to reduce its power?

Would you?

THE FAB FIVE

The well-known rumor about Ban's impending appointment at the end of his hard-driving 2006 campaign for the job was that the P-5 was lusting for a low-profile secretary general who would follow orders and not criticize the "Perfect 5". The P-5 don't like anyone calling attention to their imperfections. Ban, rumor had it, would be a less opinionated SG — or would at least express his opinions more, as it were, diplomatically.

Over at #3 Sutton Place to ask him, and the tall guard meets me at the black door and I am told he is upstairs.

There he is, in his chair, waiting, reading something — probably some top-secret report sitting atop his private study up on the third floor that is yet unseen by me.

I guess I am a few minutes late, actually. Those heavy thoughts about UN Security Council reform must have weighed me down and slowed my walk across town. But he would never say anything about that.

I start: "When in 2007 you came in, it had been widely rumored that the P-5 in particular wanted a secretary general who would be more secretary and less general. Did you hear that about what was wanted? And did you resent the implication?"

I figure we might as well go straight to it, not beat around the bush.

He is a little cool when answering: "I don't believe that of the U.S. or the other P-5, the most powerful and the most responsible members of the Security Council. They should have been much more interested in selecting a secretary general who would be capable of handling both global issues and managerial issues. And I personally believe that any secretary general should be a person who possesses such capacities."

"Both?"

"Both ... *both* capacities."

"Exterior and interior?"

He nods: "Exterior and interior: I had built up my global leadership capacity as a foreign minister and I have also built up extensive managerial capacities after having served 37 years in Korean public service. So I thought that I had both capacities and that's why they picked me."

That's not what insiders were saying about Ban. But there's no sense pushing it any more. He has said what he is going to say.

Me trying this: "But since you've been in office, have you had any member of the P-5 say anything, like you really need to not do such-and-such a [foreign] trip, or you really need to stay home more, or house-clean more, or reform more?"

"No, no, no. I'm doing things on my own and nobody has told me anything like that. I think we are working on a very cooperative and mutual respect basis."

That response sounds a little like he's dealing with five Syrian Assads.

"But regarding your relations with the P-5. From day one, were they great and they're still great? Or actually have they gotten better too?"

"I think we are working as a great team."

Hmm ... we are obviously in dicey territory. Let's try it another way.

"You said to me, when we had lunch in Los Angeles in 2006, before your appointment, something like, 'Without having a good relationship with America and with other big powers, I, we the UN, would have no place to stand.' Right?"

"Yeah."

Like, so, what about it?

"That is a very frank and honest assessment of your power. It suggests that your power is largely limited to what you can get the big powers to agree to do. One criticism of you could be that you're too, um, timid and cautious in those relationships. And the fact of the matter is that the SG's office has a moral or secular pope kind of standing, so there are times that you should go beyond that mandate."

Ban stares straight ahead, toward the window overlooking the East River. I'll bet there are days on this job when he'd like to jump into it — or push someone in it, wearing cement overshoes.

He answers: "When I said that U.S. support is crucial to the UN, that was on the political and financial support point. The U.S. pays 22 percent of the regular budget and 27 percent of peacekeeping operations. If your U.S. does not pay at the regular time, then the UN's operational capacity would be very constrained. And its political support is also very important. So when I said this frankly, there were concerns raised among my senior advisors that 'you should not say so', but I couldn't hide all these facts, the reality. So I said it many times, and that might have helped in my working closely with the U.S. administration. That does not mean that I am always cautious or timid in my relationship with the U.S. I've been speaking very clearly, and I used to have differences of opinion with the U.S. secretary of state, or, you know, even the U.S. president — ones that we had to reconcile and discuss through exchanges of views. That's what I've been doing. Of course, there are many other important countries, such as the other permanent Security Council members."

> When the permanent members, the five members, or P-5, have common views, the UN can be more successful, in most cases. When they are divided, you cannot produce effective results, so you have to draw lessons from that.

"Right." I look at one of my video cameras, as if for a little support.

"When the permanent members, the five members, or P-5, have common views, the UN can be more successful, in most cases. When they are divided, you cannot produce effective results, so you have to draw lessons from that."

I look at him for a few seconds. What I am hearing is what you are reading. I wait to see if there is anything else.

"That's what I can tell you, at this time," he says.

He doesn't mention the Peking option for obvious reasons. Power is inherently territorial and any secretary general might worry that wanting more might be perceived as wishing to see others have less, especially the Fab Five.

Slowly, then. Quietly, please. Do not be too obvious when exercising options. Right, secretary, not general.

No charisma please, I'm Korean!

BIT OF BOLTON

One big critic of the UN is its biggest financial supporter — the United States. During the years of the Bush administration, the U.S. invaded Iraq against the consensus wish of the Security Council, and — almost as bad from a UN perspective — assigned State Department official John Bolton, a notorious critic of the UN, to New York as U.S. ambassador to the UN. Before long he became Bush's bad boy at the UN. He seemed to love the role; it seemed as if few others did.

Before moving onto other issues, I ask the secretary general to look at a newspaper review of a book by former U.S. Vice President Dick Cheney (*In My Time: A Personal and Political Memoir, 2011*). In that quarrelsome tone which Cheney adopted as a distinctive style, he chose to raise credibility and experience issues about former Secretary of State Condi Rice, especially regarding North Korea. The attack felt like a gotta-get-even thing. Though I am no partisan of Rice, she seemed like a class act, from Stanford University, who worked hard to do a good job on behalf of a president who was no foreign-policy genius even when he was paying attention. I try to entice Ban to comment.

The UNSG, of course, is reluctant to get involved in trash talk of any kind (though who knows what he says in private to Soon-taek!). So he slides into a smooth, even, careful tone: "She's a nice lady and I think she liked me. We respected each other, and she had accumulated her experiences during her terms as national security advisor and as secretary of state. I didn't think at any time that she was inexperienced. No, I don't believe so. She was quite firm. Firm. Determined."

"Was she naïve about North Korea?"

He is still looking at the newspaper article while answering. His voice now gets a slight edge to it: "No, she understood everything. She understood everything on North Korea, especially how North Korea behaved, because she had already been national security advisor, and she had been with President Bush a long time before that."

Was there a mean sexist edge to our former vice president's views on Rice?

Ban wisely avoids that swamp and continues with the positive: "I am very much grateful to her. You see, I started my term as foreign minister with Colin Powell. So I started smoothly with the Bush administration. When I first visited Washington as foreign minister, President Bush received me, unexpectedly. It was very unusual that a U.S. president receives a foreign minister from any country. I was told that even the foreign secretaries of big powers like the United Kingdom and France are not received by a U.S. president. But the United States' government [had a] strong wish to improve the relationship with [South Korea]. Then Colin Powell stepped down. Condi Rice was appointed, and she was quite instrumental in my election. Of course, you know, she was not in a position to say anything publicly, that the U.S. would support Ban Ki-moon's candidature, but to my mind, Condi Rice helped a lot, and she liked me; so too did John Bolton, then the U.S. ambassador."

"He liked you, too?"

"Oh, he liked me."

"Wow. Maybe you should be a politician!"

Bolton had a short and stormy run (2005–2006) as U.S. ambassador to the UN. He was mainly known for frequently — and successfully — drawing attention to himself with a patented abrasive style. "There is no such thing as the United Nations," he once memorably proclaimed. "There is only the international community." He also said: "The Secretariat building in New York has 38 storeys. If you lost 10 storeys today, it wouldn't make a bit of difference." (Actually, there are 39, but that's close enough.) He has also pointedly declaimed that the secretary general works for the member states — period.

Ban would never say it publicly, but part of his own personality appreciates blunt-speaking. He just doesn't believe in the public display of the same. But somewhere in his Korean soul I will bet there is a bit of Bolton.

The SG adding: "I had had a previous relationship with him. That was when he was at the State Department under Bush Senior as president. I was deputy chief of the South Korean mission, and I knew him at the time. When he stepped down [as UN ambassador], and when he was not in the government, still, the Korean mission had contact with him and would invite him to receptions."

Bolton had also said: "The United Nations can be a useful instrument of American foreign policy." We remember that Ban wishes member states would take a broader, more global view of the usefulness of the UN.

Ban continuing: "At that time, our president was Roh Moo-hyun. I tried very hard as the president's diplomatic advisor to improve the relationship between the U.S. and Korea. Of course, South Korea and the U.S. is a strategic alliance partnership, but depending upon who is sitting in the White House or the Blue House, the relationship dimension used to be different, and I really wanted to help President Roh … that is what I paid a lot of attention to as a foreign minister. On this, Condi Rice helped a lot."

Me saying: "The first time I met you was after you'd spent almost a week with Condi Rice in South Korea."

He remembers indeed: "She had a very good visit to Korea. Then, when I ran for secretary general of the United Nations, she was one of the strongest supporters of my candidacy."

"Did you get along with Bolton? Is his bark worse than his bite?"

"I know how people view John Bolton, but he was, I think, a reasonable person. When it comes to the real substance of diplomacy, he is quite tough and conservative. But, you know, after long debate and exchange of views, we were able to agree upon many things."

THE BEGINNING OF TROUBLE

We take a break and walk over to the Library, which is to the left of the large staircase … a dark room intense with mahogany and velvet-lined photo frames, and one large and hilarious framed picture. It's the cover of a March 2007 *NEWSWEEK,* and on the cover is a picture of a studious looking Ki-moon, newly installed, and here is the cover line: "Why This Man Will Fail!"

He loves showing this. He's too diplomatic to make the point, of course, but the fact is that for all his imperfections and all the UN's shortcomings, it is fair to say that at this moment anyway, arguably we are both doing better than *NEWSWEEK.*

I say: "So no matter what your personality, I mean, you can bluster in front of the cameras, but, as you would say, if you don't have the P 5 behind you … right?"

"You need to be always a man of reason. Some people say, well, you are re-elected, and you don't need to care about permanent members of the Security Council, so why don't you do things on your own say-so?"

So, why not?

"That is the beginning of trouble. I don't want to create

any trouble. Even while I am very much aware of my future as a second-term secretary general, even then, the position of P-5 is very important. Being conscious of that, I have been quite the straightforward person in my feelings and dealings with the P-5. Simply, people are not aware of how I carry out my duty, how I do business with the member states of the UN, including the P-5. I always try to speak in very straightforward terms. But it is in a private discussion, through private discussion, that [this approach] in reality is more helpful."

We head back to the reception room.

I ask: "But what would be the ideal composition of the Security Council? Obviously, the way it is now is an anachronism."

Ban looks at me as if he now wonders whether I have been listening very carefully.

"I believe that I would not comment on whether the P-5's veto power is a reasonable or necessary one, but this is a fact of life. Then what I can tell you is that trying to add one more or two more permanent member states with the veto power, that may not work out — however sincere or ardent."

"So, permanent members without veto?"

"I think that's a possibility."

"Right. So who are we to add?"

He looks at me again like I am crazy: "That's a very sensitive issue. How many members should be added as permanent members? As you know there are four countries, the so-called G-4 countries, that have been working very hard to become permanent members. But again that should be determined by the member states. Then, if we need to change the composition of the Security Council, we need to think about a reasonable length for serving the Council as a member, even with the sense that this [G-4] is a permanent member."

He is alluding to some compromise so that Brazil, Germany, India and Japan might ascend to second-tier, semi-permanent seats, in some dynamic new formula. Almost everyone acknowledges that it may well prove impossible for anyone to get the same status as the current P-5, which have the "veto" and their everlasting seats at the historic horseshoe table (*Thank you Uncle Joe,,,*).

But as a compromise, there has been discussion about creating a new class of seats for the G-4 powers that would feature greatly longer terms than at present — in one formulation for as long as nine years. This would be an improvement on the current system of non-permanent seats that allow only two-year terms.

Me saying: "Everyone knows Security Council reform would be a good idea. Probably a very good idea, but if I were one of the 5 Ps, I would surely say, the heck with reform, I have a nice situation here, I don't want to lose power."

He smiles at me. A few seconds tick off.

Then: "I cannot say that. But you may say that."

I laugh.

He laughs a little, too, saying again: "I cannot say that. But you may say that."

Ban tells of a short trip the other day to nearby Glen Cove, on the classy north shore of Long Island, for a quiet meeting with key members.

"About 60 ambassadors were gathered in retreat form — headed by the president of the General Assembly — to discuss Security Council reform. There I told them that the Security Council reform discussion has been ongoing for at least the last 20 years in an open-ended working group, what we call OEWG [Open Ended Working Group], like this."

Ban stops and smiles and looks out at the window overlooking the dirty river.

"And I made a comparison to driving a car. Member states who have been talking about this reform — it is something like driving a car, with your gear positioned in a neutral position, and you push the accelerator as hard as you can. The RPM would go to 4,000, 5,000, 6,000 … a lot of noise, engine sound very dynamic … but the car has not moved even an inch, because you have positioned it in neutral."

I smile. That sounds about right.

"Then I said something like: People were listening to your effort but not with a lot of interest. Only recently, three years ago, after strong criticism, you have pushed to the car's first gear. That means you have brought the issue to the General Assembly, out from the Open Ended Working Group. Now the General Assembly is in a formal negotiations format — okay, that was good. Everybody had expectations. Then in first gear, you've been pushing down the accelerator but also pushing down the brake at the same time. So the car would move less than a mile per hour … less than a mile an hour in speed! With this speed, where do you want to go?"

"At a mile an hour…"

"Yes. [The issue for them was that] almost three quarters of our current UN membership were not members when the Security Council was established. Then is it fair to base your work on the framework which once reflected 25 percent of membership [when the UN was founded and had but 51 members]? It's unjust, unfair."

"This was the theme of the General Assembly group in Glen Cove?"

"Right."

"Their motive for Security Council reform?"

"To push."

"But as you say, they're in first gear with their foot on the brake."

"Yeah."

"Is there anything you can do?"

Ban shakes his head as if asking for divine intervention: "Kofi Annan really wanted to do something. He established a high level panel composed of eminent persons. As a foreign minister, I was called to that panel. He made proposals to the General Assembly for reform of the Security Council, which only deepened the divide … and led to no decisions. It only deteriorated the already sensitive division of the member states. So I told Kofi Annan that I'm very cautious about this … It's a member states' issue, so this is member states' work. It's not the proper work of a secretary general. I will take a facilitating role, making a good atmosphere. But after this, you [member states in the General Assembly] must make this happen."

"Is that because you don't want to waste your energy on something that's going to be a big fat zero?

"You mean Security Council reform?"

"Right."

He nods vigorously, he does agree: "I have no intention of doing that."

"Of getting involved at a high level…"

He nods.

"Because it's going to be a zero."

"It will end up, probably, a failure. In fact there is a group working on this matter. This facilitator was appointed two years ago. Three years ago, Afghanistan's ambassador, Zahir Tanin, had been working, but without making any progress. This has to be member state driven, not secretary general driven."

And that, dear reader, would appear to be that. Utopia will have to wait.

UNJUST TO JAPAN

"Let me ask you this: If I was foreign minister of South Korea, and I wanted to stay popular with domestic constituencies, I would not advocate that Japan became a permanent member of the Council. But if I were a former South Korean foreign minister who became SG, I would maybe see the issue from a different perspective and say, well, it would probably be a good thing for Japan to be a member of the Council. Of course, it's probably not going to happen but it'd be a good thing. Would that be your position?"

"My position has been a little bit different from being a South Korean. Even though I didn't say that it's a good idea if Japan became a permanent member, I said, I'm aware of the aspiration of the Japanese people to serve as a permanent member of the Council. Japan is the number two financial contributor to the UN. Japan has been contributing to peace and security, it has been a model in human rights. I've been saying only something nice. That's what I can do at this time."

"That's as far as you can go."

"Right. But, for any country, I'm not supposed to say anything. Even though it may be India, Brazil, South Africa or Germany who are so-called aspirants … they are called aspirants."

"Right, right, because if you supported X, then country Y is going to be angry with you."

"Oh yes, yes."

"Right, and there's nothing in it for you."

"A national leader — an Obama or Cameron — they are able to say so. Because they are national governments, they can have their own preference about whatever country should become a new permanent member."

His position is clear. It's not going to happen. Many things that should happen do not. This is probably one of them. Call it the real world. Or call it excessive pessimism: He assumes nothing can be done.

What's scary is that, either way, he is probably right.

There is no good way to calibrate in quantity an injustice or unfairness. It's as unfair for India as it's unfair for Japan as it's unfair for Brazil and so on. But precisely because of the tortured Korea-Japan relationship, and the physical proximity of the two countries, fates so intertwined, Ban probably feels Japan's pain more than anyone else's.

He won't be quoted to that effect, of course. But he has a huge sense of the need for South Korea to rise above the past and leave it behind. Without that, it is hard to envision the two powerful economies doing more than co-existing. We recall that Ban worked hard as foreign minister to deepen ties with Tokyo, going back to his big effort in 2005. The late Kim Dae-jung, former South Korean president who in 2000 received the Nobel Peace Prize for his 'Sunshine Policy' efforts toward North Korea, also worked for this. Ban admired DJ, as he was known, even though Ban had to take the rap for the famous fiasco of misunderstanding involving the Bush administration.

Relations with Japan may be the trickiest of all of South Korea's foreign-relations portfolios. In domestic politics, memories of the wartime 'comfort women' are never far below the surface, a readily available populist button for any Korean politician to push. But on the level of smart international relations, Seoul needs good relations with Tokyo, which is also a U.S. ally, and a counterweight to North Korea, if not also in theory, to China — should that nearby Goliath turn ugly.

Ban is not afraid to raise the apology issue over Japan's wartime behavior, believed in Asia to be insufficiently atoned for. But unlike many Korean politicians he's not of the view that the Japanese must bow and scrape every other day to make for fruitful relations.

"During my visit to Japan in 2010 — that marked the 100th year of the Japanese annexation of Korea — I talked to very senior Japanese government officials, to say that I think Japan should take a genuinely sincere attitude toward the Korean people on this occasion; that while we should not talk too much about the past, the best way of putting the past behind us is to look forward to the future for another 100 years, so that then they should express their very sincere apology by the prime minster, by the government. And that's what they did, that's what they did."

Ban hopes that all of Asia will stop abusing the apology card.

"At the same time, the Korean government itself must negotiate [in good faith] with the Japanese. As a South Korean citizen but also in my capacity as secretary general, I want to see a very harmonious, constructive and forward-looking relationship between Japan and Korea, one that helps peace and stability in Northeast Asia. That's what the UN secretary general wants."

> ...the Korean government itself must negotiate [in good faith] with the Japanese. As a South Korean citizen but also in my capacity as secretary general, I want to see a very harmonious, constructive and forward-looking relationship between Japan and Korea, one that helps peace and stability in Northeast Asia.

In August 2010, Ban became the first UNSG to attend the Hiroshima Peace Memorial Service.

"It was the most profoundly moving experience. Meeting with survivors who are called *hibakusha* — they are called the *hibakusha* in Japanese — really made me very saddened and moved, but at the same time I was much encouraged to see their fortitude and courage. I had never experienced this kind of thing, and I was not there to talk about who did what during the war."

Ban accepts that political cynicism is as widespread in Asia as anywhere.

"The most important thing in being there was to demonstrate again my commitment, to draw attention to the fact that we still have a world full of nuclear weapons. I really wanted to help those survivors whose time is very limited now ... they are mostly over 75 years old, 80 and 85 years old even. During their limited time, if they could see a world without any fear of nuclear weapons ... that was my hope. So I decided to go. Nobody recommended it to me, and I knew that there were sensitivities on the part of some other nuclear-weapon states, particularly in the American government.

But I think my visit there seemed to have encouraged the U.S., Great Britain and France to send their special envoys for the first time. That created momentum for them to change their position [of non-participation]. I feel a sense of achievement and pride about this."

> The most important thing in being there [the Hiroshima Peace Memorial Service] was to demonstrate again my commitment, to draw attention to the fact that we still have a world full of nuclear weapons.

The trip served a second purpose. As a *Korean* diplomat, Ban feels it his moral obligation as foreign minister and now as UNSG to accord Japan respect. Rather than harp on the war crimes and compensation issues, as do many Korean politicians, irresponsibly playing what the Japanese understandably regard as the 'apology card', Ban goes to the Hiroshima peace memorial observance.

I flash back to a meeting in 2005, when he was foreign minister. This was at the gorgeous Chosun Hotel in downtown Seoul. I say to him: "I remember your comment on the subject of East Asian diplomacy the first time we met. You said that a South Korean foreign minister needs to rise above the region's pettiness. And so it is incumbent on Japan and South Korea to be adults and to work through problems, and that as foreign minister you would have an open-door policy towards your counterpart in Tokyo. You said you knew that if you traveled there on a diplomatic mission [in 2005] you would be welcomed with open arms by the Japanese foreign minister. And I remember that two weeks later you gave a speech like that, and I wrote a column about it and it ran on the op-ed page of *The Japan Times* and I said it was a perfect example of good diplomacy."

Ban smiles. He remembers everything he deems important. Sometimes people who talk less save some interior space to remember more.

HAPPY TRICKSTER

He played a little trick on Tokyo and Seoul for the benefit of the Haitian relief effort after the terrible Caribbean earthquake.

The details come to us courtesy of Korean Ambassador Park In-kook. He knows Ban well from their long career run as foreign service officers. It goes back to the 2010 earthquake in Haiti that almost tipped this ill-starred island country into the Caribbean for good. The casualties were horrendous but the international relief effort much less so.

Ban, by this time, had firmly established his parachute-into-Mother-Nature's-latest-disaster reputation: "You have a disaster? Watch out! Here comes BKM on the next available flight!"

And to Haiti he flew, on one occasion with former President Bill Clinton, who for a time practically made Haiti his personal adopted disaster area.

For Ban, though, fundraising for special needs has become part of the job, and that means, like a college president or the head of a nonprofit, you work the phones. So from his secret study on the third floor of his residence at night, he telephones Lee Myung-bak in Seoul, where it is morning — as he is dialing long distance for dollars.

"MB", as he is often called, was the then incumbent president of the formally named Republic of Korea. On the first pitch the SG elicits an immediate pledge of a mere million dollars. At first the gracious Ban says nothing more than a warm thank you, but then the puckish Ban kicks in, so before hanging up the SG casually mentions that the Japanese have already pledged a cool five million for Haiti relief.

Well, by kimchi-golly! No hot-blooded Korean politician can permit Korea to be topped like that, so in the flash of seconds Seoul is good for another four million.

Whereupon Ban then shamelessly dials the prime minister in Tokyo and says, guess what? MB just kicked in five million for Haitian relief. So what is the Japanese PM to say? After all, Japan is a richer country than Korea and it can't just give *only* as much as the Koreans…

Then Ban calls Seoul back and says, guess what? Tokyo is up to 10 million, you got anything left?

I am back to the second floor reception room with the SG and I relate Ambassador Park's story and Ban's face brightens greatly and he laughs: "Oh yes, that's what I've been doing!"

Me following: "You do little things like that every week?"

Oh, sometimes, he suggests.

"But that's not been in the press, right?"

"Oh, no no no. I don't want to make these things into press stories."

And he sometimes wonders why he has had an image problem with the media!

STEP UP, KOREA AND CHINA

The story gives me the opportunity to ask if he has any criticisms of his native country. I say: "South Korea's come a long way. It has the big bucks to play in the big leagues now."

Ban thinks this through carefully, then says: "We have come quite a long way, but we need to do more. South Koreans, while achieving rapid economic development, have made errors, many errors, repeated errors. If we would have been able to prevent these errors, we might have been able to develop much faster and much more fully. But I think it was some kind of learning process and we should be proud of what we have achieved."

"Absolutely."

"But in terms of full globalization, full maturity, having a mature political and social system, I think we need to do more. I need to be very frank about that."

"By we, you mean South Korea?"

"South Korea."

"So even though you're secretary general of all 193 nations, there is a part in your heart and brain that's still reserved for your homeland, isn't it?"

"Yes. Look at what the United States is doing, paying at least one-fifth of the financial dues of the United Nations. Japan and most of the European countries ... they do take their own global share and that I really appreciate.

"Now, if I want to ask the South Korean government and people [to rise to that level], then they should make contributions commensurate with their economic development. After all, Korea was rebuilt with the help of the international community, especially with the help of the UN. For us, the UN was a beacon of hope. We can never forget that UN forces came to rescue us, which was led by the U.S., mostly; and then came the massive economic and social support from the international community. So now it is time to pay back what they have received."

"Is South Korea reluctant to do this?"

"No, no, they are willing. But they are not doing enough."

"And so you're going to cheerlead a little bit?"

"Oh yes, I've been working very hard and I've been really sometimes pounding my own home country. Finally they have tripled their official development assistance, but this is still not enough! Even with tripling this amount, that means Korea has been doing relatively very little. The first time I went back to Korea

I expressed my frank views to the Korean public. Perhaps they were surprised to hear the secretary general speaking in such a candid way.

"I told them I was ashamed of being a Korean, sitting as SG, when the Korean delegation pledged a certain [limited] amount of money for world food security issues. When there was a summit meeting on world food security in 2008, Korea could have done much more. This event was convened by me, and I expressed that anger. The Korean government took it very seriously, the Korean media took it very seriously and reported it. The Korean people hadn't understood the real story about this, and so it was then that Korean development assistance tripled. I still think that, considering growing Korean economic power, they should do even more."

Ban also has advice for another — much larger — rising Asian power.

He remarks: "China needs to harmonize with international standards, but they have taken their own Chinese way … you cannot just disregard rapidly growing Chinese economic power. As I mentioned, I hope that South Korea will do more globally. But considering just the sheer size of the population and economic wealth of both China and India, they have become, like already, global powers. So I do hope that with all its economic growth China will become more mature."

"More mature?"

"Mature in their democratic ways and in their dealing with

international matters."

I am worried too. "But look at China recently with the People's Liberation Army saying all the water around it — the so-called South China Sea — is our pond, our lake, a seeming assertion of territoriality that I don't think international law would support. In response the U.S. upped the profile of its Pacific Fleet. Does that worry you? Do you maybe see China as very immature, and of course the U.S. sometimes seems all too ready to do something militarily. Are you worried about that?"

He shakes his head: "All in all I'm sure that China will adapt very quickly to the international community's standards. That's what I hope. Then it will be much easier for the international community to realize resolution of all the disputes involving China."

One so hopes this prognostication is embraced by history.

"I once asked you why you think Hollywood so loves the Dalai Lama and, of course, for you it's a no-win thing to get involved in. But it's interesting that you looked at me and said something like: *Part of the problem is that although China is surging economically, its diplomacy is still at a lower level of evolution, that the sophistication of the diplomacy has not really kept pace with the dynamic evolution of the economy.* Now that's a very interesting thought ... about how China has been slow to change diplomatically and develop more sophisticated responses to international issues."

Ban nods in agreement but adds: "They have recently been trying to maintain a higher profile in the diplomatic area. One time when I was attending and negotiating on climate change, it was basically China who spoke out, not only for the interest of the Chinese national situation but also for the benefit of developing countries. So I think many developing countries were standing behind China, and China basically spoke out for their cause. So you will see levels of difference in their diplomatic skills.

"But for me as secretary general, it would be very important to maintain a close relationship with China and get support from the Chinese government. As much as it is true to say almost nothing can be done without strong support of the United States, it is also true to say that without Chinese support, cooperation and participation, it would be extremely difficult to have a smooth functioning of the United Nations."

> But for me as secretary general, it would be very important to maintain a close relationship with China ... without Chinese support, cooperation and participation, it would be extremely difficult to have a smooth functioning of the United Nations.

"Would you say that 20 or 30 years ago the secretary general's most important client was the U.S., but today China is as important as the U.S.?"

"Almost."

"Almost as important?"

"Almost as important."

WHAT PART SO EVER YOU TAKE UPON
YOU, PLAY THAT AS WELL AS YOU CAN
AND MAKE THE BEST OF IT.

– Utopia

Parting Dreams

Shrinking turtle… cat and canary … slippery deal seal

OF THE THREE rooms on the second floor of #3 Sutton Place, Manhattan, the smallest is the brightest. They call it the second floor study, with a desk for the secretary general that, of course, has to have the required map of the world hanging over it. After five years on the job, he probably knows rather well where everything is.

There, he poses graciously for a picture, but the desk seems too orderly and fluffed. Yes, the real deal has to be the very private study up one flight. Will we ever get to see it?

We settle in, he on the small sofa, near the white mock fireplace and the large green plant to my right. The mini-video cameras are arranged. It is a Saturday morning and, unusually, the SG is without a tie. But he is in a sports jacket.

SHRINKING TURTLE

The subject today is one dear to his heart — North Korea.

Me saying: "In South Korea, in addition to the pressure of having to be almost a role model for the entire Korean nation, of course, there arises the second question, which is: Why did Ban

Ki-moon do nothing about North Korea in his first term? Can he do something about North Korea in his second term?"

But a better way of asking that question is: What circumstances might arise requiring your involvement? We will get to that eventually.

Ban: "First of all, my understanding is that North Koreans also supported my election. For my second term, they supported again, even though they didn't speak publicly. That's what they told me privately: 'Mr. Secretary General, you know that we support you, but for all these understandable reasons, we are not going to speak out publicly.' So I said, 'That's more than enough.'"

"They didn't want to publicly support you. They thought it might hurt, huh?" It is interesting that they even bothered to express their support. I cannot imagine that Ban's first instinct was to ask his media staff to trumpet out a press release.

"They came to me, and they extended an invitation to visit: 'You are welcome any time.' Then, as you know, during 2010, the situation turned dramatically negative, through the Cheonan incident and the shelling of Yeongpyeong Island. That has constrained my position. The role of the secretary general in the case of these kinds of 'hot' issues gets complicated."

Ban takes his gaze off me and focuses on his tea.

He says: "Once there was a forum date agreed [in 2009]."

"There was?!"

"Oh, yes, yes. I consulted with the South Korean president, and also the U.S. State Department, Secretary Clinton, and there was agreement that I needed to go. Then, suddenly, the North Koreans changed their mind. And then I changed my mind. I was engaging heavily on the climate change issue in Copenhagen. I couldn't take any time out for this. After that was over, when there was agreement on the date, then the North Koreans changed *their* mind. So two opportunities were lost there. One by me, and one by the North Koreans."

"You delayed because you were tied up at Copenhagen, and then, was it after that that the North Koreans got cold feet?"

"Yeah, that's right. Well, it's not cold feet — but they preferred that I should come a little bit later. Then, later, I understood why."

"Health issues of the maximum leader?"

Ban wouldn't respond to that but it may have hit the mark: "The normal North Korean way of doing business is that when they have some big issues, they always concentrate on one issue, and then they do not accept foreign guests. I think Kim Jong-il must've had some bigger issues at that time."

"So here you are, a Korean who makes it to the absolute top of world diplomacy — and the Korean War is still not over. It must really get to your gut, to your heart, and if something horrible happens again on the Korean Peninsula, from your perspective it would be almost the most painful stupidity that you could imagine, short of worldwide nuclear war, right?"

Ban churns a little inside, you can feel it. Germany is united but Korea is not — how stupid and unfair is that?

"It is very sad and as a Korean citizen I feel really ashamed. It's a shame that the Korean people could not have resolved this conflict between the South and North even after 65 years of the outbreak of the Korean War. There have been many initiatives and dialogues between South and North, but because of the conflict of ideologies … Even after the end of the Cold War, there was good momentum created through South-North summit meetings on two occasions but those momentums were not sustained for various reasons. But largely it is because of North Korea's inflexibility and its closed-ness and their very unique system."

"Very unique system?" That's got to be a true diplomat's way of depicting North Korea, right? But you could almost see the sneer in his eyes.

He continues, his eyes looking downwards, as if truly sad at the sight below: "The system is totally closed and it has one-man rule and total isolatedness of North Korea … that makes them fearful of being exposed, being open to the outside world. Opening themselves, they might have thought, well, that it is the end of their regime. Therefore, the more globalization has progressed, the more they have become shrunken in fear, like the neck of a turtle … the turtle's neck shrinking inside. They are just simply afraid. This is why the Korean conflict still continues."

Time-out here! That shrinking turtle neck is a fitting image, no?

"But you read in world history, of the Thirty Years War, of the Hundred Years War, and you wonder, how come people fight for 100 years! But now I can easily understand why. And so this Korean war has continued 65 years now. So how long will this continue, how soon will we be able to resolve this and become united?

"This is a very serious and fundamental challenge to me. As secretary general, I feel a much, much greater sense of responsibility [on this issue], and my hope is to be able to contribute in whatever way to facilitate the unification process or, if that's not possible, then just even prevent any unpredictable, uncontrollable situation from happening."

"Such as the Cheonan incident."

In March of 2010, a small North Korean submarine, without warning, fired a torpedo at the Cheonan in the Yellow Sea, killing 104 sailors and staff on the South Korean naval vessel. North Korea denied responsibility, but few nations bought that.

"What the heck happened there? Was it a rogue element of the military that was the trigger?"

Ban nods: "Yes, yes."

"That's what I thought."

"That has been one of the most difficult moments for me and what kind of a role I should play in this threat to international peace and security. I'm sure this situation can change for the better and I will try to seize any opportunity for momentum."

The Cheonan attack was taken up by the Security Council. Ban, perhaps surprisingly, took a high profile. He says: "What should be the role of the secretary general who is a South Korean? That really put me in a very difficult position, but I [coughs and reaches for some water]…"

I remind him that on this occasion his low-profile Asian style seemed to have been thrown out the window.

"Oh yes. I spoke out that the Security Council should [meet formally and] take necessary measures. The finding of the international joint investigative mission on the Cheonan sinking was compelling and decisive — it was done by North Koreans. No doubt in my mind."

He continues: "Therefore the Security Council should take necessary measures, corresponding to the gravity and the seriousness of the situation. Now to that of course the North Koreans protested."

He won't say it, but the tender sensitivities of the government in Pyongyang are not topmost on his list of diplomatic concerns.

"As the secretary general, I have to take rather sensitive positions, but I was convinced that these [attacks] were done by North Koreans. When I was having a press conference, there were many questions, and I made a very strong statement that the Security Council should take necessary measures. The role of the

> As a Korean citizen I feel really ashamed ... that the Korean people could not have resolved this conflict between the South and North even after 65 years of the outbreak of the Korean War ... Even after the end of the Cold War, there was good momentum created through South-North summit meetings on two occasions but those momentums were not sustained for various reasons.

secretary general, according to the UN Charter, is not to demand the Security Council take action, but I can raise any issue to the attention of the Council."

"You can call a meeting."

"Yes. Raise the issue to the attention of the Council in accordance with the Charter. Then there was some criticism whether I went beyond this Charter mandate. So I said, don't mess around with all these questions. I'm talking about my motherland. Of course, the secretary general should not mention his motherland routinely, but in this case people immediately understood, and they didn't make anything major out of this."

"One reason for that was that you had been trying, up to that point, to be scrupulous about being an *international* secretary general, and not a Korean secretary general, so you were really trying to stay above criticism on that point."

Ban nods: "Then, of course, North Koreans protested officially — official letter of correspondence, and one day, somebody came, at a very senior level from the DPRK, and protested orally. So I told them, 'Please, don't regard me as secretary general coming from South Korea. I'm not acting as a South Korean secretary general; I'm acting as secretary general. Period.'"

"Where there's a violation of peace and security…"

He nods: "I just firmly defended my position. Now there is some misperception, in the international community, that in every issue the United Nations should be there, but it's not the case. When there is some existing framework of solution, then, normally, we do not get involved directly. When there is a Six-Party framework, when there is a bilateral dialogue between North and South Korea, my role would be to facilitate and encourage the Six-Party and bilateral dialogue.

"That is why I have been trying to refrain from directly getting involved in that. You see, it was 17 or so years ago when the last secretary general [Boutros Boutros-Ghali] visited North Korea. Then, during 10 years of Kofi Annan, he never visited North Korea. During that time, even though there were some ups and downs, there were continuous exchanges and some cooperation between South and North Korea, so Kofi Annan didn't see much need to get himself involved. When I first arrived here, I was coming directly from the position of foreign minister. To any South Korean foreign minister, North Korea is *the* issue, and the strategic alliance and relationship with the U.S. is a most important concern."

"It used to be almost 100 percent of the job. You changed it with all your travels but—"

"Hundred percent of the job, yes, yes. When I came, I really wanted to have some internal discussion on North Korean issues, but senior advisors here, they were not ready, and they would advise me, 'Well, this is not a hot issue here. There's not much the SG can do.' Then, six months later, I said, upon my insistence, we need at least to discuss the Korean peninsula. But the priority on this issue has always been at the bottom of the UN concerns list. So when that tragedy arose, I really wanted to take a certain role.

"Now, during my second term … you should know that I have

a standing invitation. Whenever there is appropriate agenda and timing, I'm going to visit. You cannot wait indefinitely."

"Right, and you know, you have to go at least once, or when you step down, you'll kill yourself."

"Of course, of course."

"In your heart ... our current secretary general happens to be Korean, not a Korean who happens to be secretary general. So in your heart?"

"Yes, on this, I always feel very heavy in my heart."

Me saying: "And you know, it's interesting. There is almost no story to me in 16 years of writing columns and books about Asia that is more amazing than the rise of South Korea — divided by war, devastated for decades, occupied by the Japanese, but then you wake up and it's the 12th largest economy. And if it had gotten a geopolitical break and become a united Korea, what would it be? It might really be the Germany of Asia. Even as it stands now, divided from the North, this is a country that is enormously accomplished. You have the brilliant Olympic skater Kim Yu-na and all of the tremendous Korean musicians and so on, and now a Korean gentleman as the UNSG. This is such a capstone for South Korea ... It must really feel good as long as you don't look North and there you see the Dark Ages or whatever. Now God comes down to you one day and I don't know whether it's God or Allah or Confucius or whoever..."

We chuckle.

"...and says, 'you know, Mr. Ban Ki-moon, I've been watching the way the press has been mean to you but you really have been doing a good job as secretary general, and every month you're getting better and better, and in your second term you might prove to be one of the best ever, who knows? So I'm going to give you a wish, I'm going to let you solve any crisis that you want, you just tell me which one, would it be North Korea?' "

Ban smiles. He likes the Almighty's question, of course, and of course I rather like playing God!

"I hope that I will be able to contribute, if not solely by myself but with the help of all the international community, to resolve this issue ... that's my hope and my dream. We cannot go on like this..."

"We can't go on this way anymore. Isn't it really the end of the road?"

"It's an injustice to many North Korean citizens, our brethren who have been suffering from all this poverty and this tight control, total isolation without being able to enjoy genuine freedom and human rights."

"Or just even a decent basic standard of living."

"It's very sad."

"Now I hope you won't mind my simple minded naïveté but let's make believe that I'm the U.S. president and I call up my man DICM up there in NY to do the North Korean thing. So how could we get the so-called "grand bargain" to denuclearize North Korea and normalize its relations with the outside world — how could we get that done? Maybe I ought to go to Pyongyang with BKM.

Do you ever imagine something like that could happen?"

"There's always the possibility. Then again, I've really been ready to visit Pyongyang myself and meet with North Korean leaders, but somehow there has not been proper climate or atmosphere conducive to that happening."

"Because you don't want to go up there and come back with nothing?"

"But it's not because I didn't want to go, I'm ready to do it."

"Tomorrow?"

"Anytime, anytime!"

"Even economy class?"

He laughs: "Yes! I am ready to do it anytime and I'm sure that DPRK authorities are aware of my readiness, and I think my dialogues with them have been reasonably good. They try to respect me, and my dialogues with the North Korean UN ambassador or visiting VIPs from North Korea have always been cordial. So they try to regard me as secretary general, and according to them, even they were proud of me as a Korean serving as SG."

"They're not jealous, they're proud? Or both?"

"Maybe both." He laughs: "So that is one of my challenges; one of my big challenges as well as one of my dreams, is just to make a personal contribution to this problem."[3]

"I remember the late Warren Christopher, Bill Clinton's secretary of state, used to say when I would ask, 'Do we journalists

---

3 See David Harland, "Kosovo and the UN," *Survival.* Vol. 52, No. 5.
October-November 2010.

overrate North Korea as a serious problem?' He'd shake his head to indicate no, not at all, and say it was in the top 5 — *top 5* — of all crisis-list issues for any American president."

"Yes, it will be one of the biggest events in the recent politics in our international community if we realize the unification of both South and North Korea."

"In thinking about that kind of move, going to Pyongyang … it's such a dramatic move that even the media could understand it!"

"Korean Arab Spring?"

"Yes, yes, that's right."

"There's nowhere else to go for them."

"Yes, nowhere else to go. It has been always China [helping them] but I believe that there will be some limit for China to sustain and support North Korea given such bad behavior."

I flash back to a private briefing given me the day before by a top South Korean diplomat. He told me that the SG won't go on record but over a casual golf game or two with a top Chinese diplomat, he came to accept both the limitations on what Beijing would be willing to do actively to curb Pyongyang, as well as their basic agreement on what needs to be done. The SG thus feels all sides, according to a source who knows him, "are in the same boat, it's just that our methods and ways are different." The SG himself is almost a closet hawk, believing the firmer the allied position, the more action "we will get from them", as the diplomat put it. In his heart he detests any government that through its own fault does not feed its people. "His frustration is great," says the high-level source.

Publicly, Ban sticks with the negotiation line: "Then, for them, the only way out is to engage again with Six-Party members. That's why they say, 'Oh, let us have Six Party talks. We are ready. We are willing to declare a moratorium on nuclear production, nuclear materials and testing nuclear weapons.'"

"Credibility issues?"

"Yeah, credibility issues."

"But Seoul and Washington, not to mention Tokyo, say they have been through this Six Party talk stuff and feel that this is just more twiddling around, not getting anywhere. Are you sympathetic with Washington's position, or would you say that there's nothing to be lost by going back to the Six Party talks?"

Ban nods affirmatively. No question in his mind.

But let us put it this way: "One problem with the Six Party talks is they're not at a high enough level, and these North Korean negotiators, they're scared out of their mind to negotiate, because, as you say, negotiation is give and take. You know, I give 50 percent, and keep the 50 that I really want, and, like that, no one gets 100 percent. But they're scared to have their hands chopped off, once they go back to Pyongyang. The only way to get this thing done is at the highest level, and every time Clinton goes, or Carter goes, or Koizumi [former Japanese PM] goes, or any very high level person goes, something happens, right?"

Ban listens, but you are never going to be able to convince him of the futility of direct negotiations — no matter what the odds against success, no matter how many times they have tried and

failed, no matter how fatigued by the process all sides may be. As a
UN official intimately involved in the successful UN negotiations
over Kosovo put it to me: "He is a man for the absolutely dogged
pursuit of the no face-losing win-win, while everyone else will be
grabbing for microphones. There is no grandstanding. And he has
a huge tolerance for ambiguity." He adds: "Ban looks at history as a
river ... eventually the future emerges out of it. Patience."

Ban says: "Not as a South Korean but as secretary general, I
would recommend and support the resumption of dialogue, in
any way."

"Because you always think that that's worth doing…"

"Yes."

"No matter how endlessly tedious, no matter how seemingly
pointless, you never know. Is that your view?"

He resurrects the Asian way of thinking about progress:
"Americans, and some Europeans, care for productivity and results
but, practically speaking, for this type of negotiation, involving
parties who have been separated during the last 65 years, you need
to get them to negotiations, in any way. Otherwise, if you just
look at each other without talking, then there's no way for moving
each other."

"But the American position might be, 'Well, we're just going
to sit around the same damn table, and they're going to read
their boilerplate speeches, and then we're going to ask the same
questions, you know, and the Japanese are going to grumble, and
Seoul's going to grumble and Beijing's going to say, you know,

'Keep talking, keep talking, keep talking,' and it's just one big waste of time."

"Hmm. That may be, but without dialogue, then how can you resolve this?"

In fact, there was a moment when the U.S. government was seriously considering a presidential visit to Pyongyang. This, of course, was President Clinton at the end of his second term. Says Ban: "I know that he was considering that very seriously. But there was too little time left, and George Bush was already elected President."

"Right, and Bush would have had to agree to sign off on an agreement, which he wasn't going to do."

"I think that was a missed opportunity."

"That was a missed opportunity. Rightly or wrongly, the Clinton people think they had it put together."

Ban nods: "That's right."

CAT AND CANARY

We are having a last conversation in the reception room. It takes place in late March 2012, during the first year of his second term. He is feeling chipper. Two days before, a column in the progressive London daily *The Guardian* lauded Ban's flamboyant workaholism at the UN. The headline was "Don't Blame Ban Ki-moon For All The UN's Problems."

Trying to catch him in an uptick mood, it seemed the right time to elicit some long-range thoughts.

"Now, supposing when you leave in 4.6 years or whatever it is—"

"Why 4.6? I have only done five years."

Despite everything, he sounds as if he's in no rush to leave — or worried someone will push him out.

"You have a second five but you only have 4.6 or 4.7 of it left!"

"Another four years left — right!" He seems relieved.

Here is my pitch: "Magically, in December 2016 you have left the United Nations with a 50,000 person army. Don't ask me how it happened."

This has been one of those utopian proposals (like a reformed Security Council membership structure, to reflect 2012, not 1945) that everyone agrees is one of those great ideas that will probably never happen

Ban, understandably, gestures like, Yeah right. Like my French is suddenly as elegant as that of Albert Camus.

I shake my head: "No, no, no, let us not become overly pragmatic. Imagine that God came down, Allah came down — whatever — and said this: The UN cannot go on, not be effective without something like that. Right? Just make believe it happened."

I am trying to return Ban to his teen years, the time when he met John F. Kennedy with other Red Cross scholarship students and was so inspired. But age does much to shrink a man's utopianism.

"Would that have been enough UNSG soldiers — 50,000 — to stop Assad?" The size of the regular Syrian army is estimated to be considerably more than 50,000.

Ban replies: "At this time, we have 120,000 soldiers provided by—"

Is he trying to avoid the utopian thought?

Me saying: "No, what I mean is that—"

"Right, what you mean is a standing army."

Precisely. "The UNSG as commander in chief."

His face takes on the look of a cat in sight of a canary it must have: "This is an ideal, ideal situation."

He gets it. Me again: "Right, right, supposing you had the ideal."

"When we have a standing army that can immediately be deployed to crisis scene…" This sounds so good, he seems to be sighing.

Then Ban adds: "But the UN has been considering this matter, but has not been able to agree on anything. The collective system of the UN, in its charter … it's not perfect but we have been able to manage peace and security around the world by maintaining this with 120,000 soldiers, but it takes a lot of time to mobilize soldiers and deploy. Normally it takes six months to one year. For example, in Darfur, today we have 25,000 soldiers, the largest and biggest one. It took almost two years to build it up to almost 25,000 soldiers."

And this is just for peacekeeping, a term meaning maintenance of a peaceful status quo, which all parties agree should be maintained. This is dramatically different from peacemaking. That requires the exercise of force of will against a resisting party or obstreperous parties.

"So they are peacekeeping forces, not peacemaking or peace enforcing forces, unless otherwise directed and authorized by the Security Council. So it's all peacekeeping without using heavy artillery, heavy fire. With light guns, they just stay in the middle, between the two warring parties, so that they would not engage in fighting again.

"So we are in the middle and sometimes we lose a lot of soldiers because of this. We are not authorized to enforce peace; we are authorized to take only defensive measures. It's always casualties on the part of the UN forces unfortunately."

Ban is into this now: "Ideally speaking, we need to have a standing army, so [instead] we are advising the member states to have an individual standing army [good to go], what we call a standby arrangement by the national government. For example, Bangladesh has prepared standby arrangement forces [ready to be deployed] for the peacekeeping forces. They have their own training for peacekeeping operations ... I visited there. We can have Bangladesh soldiers any time."

"Is that right?"

"Yeah. But most of the member states ... they do not have this ready for us."

This is the crux of the matter.

"Therefore, if there is any crisis, if there's any necessity for peacekeeping operations, we have to ask member states to provide their soldiers, and it takes a long time. You cannot have always Bangladesh soldiers (for all situations). Many situations need multinational forces. The UN being multilateral, we need to have a multilateral force with one command system. It's an efficiency and effectiveness problem."

"But suppose you had a 50,000-man standing army reporting to the secretary general."

"It'd be wonderful."

"Wonderful?"

"Wonderful."

"Right. But what I'm trying to say is, supposing when you are on the phone with President Assad, you can say: I have been talking with you and talking to you now for over a year, you don't listen to me. I have to tell you that power is not eternal, you're not going to be there forever, you should leave in a good way. So you're not going to leave? Then I'm going to send my 50,000-strong UN army in. Would that have been enough to do that job?"

> Many situations need multinational forces. The UN being multilateral, we need to have a multilateral force with one command system. It's an efficiency and effectiveness problem.

"I cannot say whether that would be sufficient but it would be good for the UN to have that, to maintain the situation and peace and stability."

"It would be credible then."

"Credible, credible."

"You are saying that you don't need 500,000. Yet 500 or 5,000 is too little. But then something like 40,000 or 50,000, is that the number?"

Once again, he ducks out of utopia and dives back into reality. He does seem more comfortable there.

"But at this time, no UN mission has that many. We have 15 missions, altogether totaling 120,000, the largest one is 25,000 in Darfur. Mostly 10,000, 7,000, 8,000, or sometimes 500 ... like this."

"But if you were giving your farewell speech in five years, and you had a short list of things you wished the UN to have, this would be on that list, right? However utopian, the ideal would be some kind of standing army for the UN. Is that right?"

"But during my term..."

I know what he is going to say.

I say: "It's not going to happen."

"It's not going to happen. I don't think it will happen."

"Right. But sometimes you need to go for the ideal."

"That's right. Sometimes you need to be out of the box or you need to be very ambitious. But you should be very practical. That's what I'm always saying to young people: You young people, be bold and ambitious but practical. As I told you, put your head above the clouds; that means, you should have an ideal, bold and ambitious, but have your two feet firmly on the ground."

Or sometimes when the ground beneath you is moving, maybe three.

"And move step by step. That means you need to be practical, otherwise you'll tumble, you'll fall. You'll not be able to achieve even half of what you aim. Always, my message, philosophical message to our staff, young people: Put your head above the clouds but have your two feet firmly grounded and move step by step."

"Would you welcome your successor being a woman?"

"Yes, I would. There was a strong wish from the women community when I was running for this, and it is high time the women community argued for a woman."

"Will you try to actively mentor somebody from … who's up next? Latin America? Or Europe?"

> Sometimes you need to be out of the box or you need to be very ambitious. But you should be very practical … put your head above the clouds but have your two feet firmly grounded and move step by step.

"If the usual regional rotation is respected, it should be Eastern European, but there is, again, whether an Eastern European will have that kind of standing, because many Eastern European countries have joined the European Union or NATO. But as a group, they still exist in the UN system, so there will be a strong wish from the Eastern European group that will say, 'This is our turn.' But if not, I think it would be a Western European."

"If you could, would you try and mentor someone into that position?"

"Well, I don't know that this is the position where the secretary general can mentor or not. It's, after all, an issue for the member states."

"What's your third big endgame issue? We've covered two, global warming and gender equality, and there's a third on your list, right?"

"I have to change the management of the UN. Again, I'm proud to tell you that I have changed it a lot. I *have* changed it a lot. In terms of enhancing accountability, effectiveness, efficiencies, and ethics, now there's a [new] mentality from the UN staff. There was huge opposition from among our own staff, because all these staff originate from one of the 193 member states, so they bring different backgrounds, different perspectives. It's very hard to take this composition of all these different people and make them into one organization of staff, and I don't claim that I have been successful to the level which I want to bring it to. But I'll continue to do that. During the last 65 years, the UN, with all these organizations and departments around the world, has been sort of just patched up together."

"A patchwork?"

"Yeah, a patchwork. A patchwork. That's why it's very difficult to maybe streamline all this."

"Because your job is unique, do you have a sense that the world is degrading fast, or do you have a sense that despite all the problems, international cooperation is getting a little better, there's a little more consensus, there's a little less national self-seeking? What is the direction of the world?"

"That's a fundamental question, a very important question, which may or may not find a good answer from me, or from

💬 I have to change the management of the UN. Again, I'm proud to tell you that I have changed it a lot … In terms of enhancing accountability, effectiveness, efficiencies, and ethics, now there's a [new] mentality from the UN staff. 💬

anybody else. But what I'm thinking at this time is, this world is going to be more and more complex and more difficult. The UN represents the whole international community. At the same time there is a much, much stronger sense of ownership of each and every country. There's a heightened awareness of sovereignty. Of course, sovereignty is a fundamentally important principle in the UN Charter."

What he is suggesting is that the disunited aspect of the UN is structurally embedded in the organization's originating charter.

"Then, all these difficulties are compounded by the global challenges that have been neglected by the member states, like climate change, and the consequences are approaching, fast approaching. Look at all the extreme weather patterns that we have seen most recently."

"Something's going on, right?"

"Yeah, something's going on. Then the water scarcity, food crisis, the [food] production level of every country is going down. And because of that, this distrust and conflict between the tribes and between the neighbors becomes greater, and then this becomes regional conflict … and so on.

"So the international community, or United Nations, needs to have a more effective role. It should not be called an intervention, but when it is necessary, there should in effect be an intervention. Sure, we are running here and there to provide humanitarian assistance to many people who are dying of hunger and disease. But even with humanitarian assistance, there are some countries who are trying to take ownership and limit the movement of the UN. This has really constrained our capacity."

Ban is as agitated as I have ever seen him in these sessions.

"When it comes to political matters, everybody takes strong ownership and won't give in, but when there is a serious problem, there are a lot of organizations — African Union, European Union, the League of Arab States, the Organization of Islamic Cooperation — they take their own ownership, and in a group of //, however reasonable the proposed policy, when some of the countries in such groups make noise, then nothing can be done. That is totally unfair."

You can feel his mind, as well as his emotions, racing.

"You lose ... we have lost a lot of opportunities. It's too high a price, because we could have saved a lot of people with much less money. This is what I am very concerned and troubled about. Should we continue like this?"

It's time for my own intervention. I pitch him this: "To condense it a little bit. The reality of the world is that its problems are ever mounting and, of course, becoming increasingly international, and yet the Westphalian tradition of nation-states' sovereignty has remained the same, and has really in a sense been blocking action. Is that what you're saying?"

He nods vigorously: "That's right. That's right. This is a very serious problem. The international community works normally on a consensus basis, whether it is a regional, small organization, or a big organization. But the true meaning of consensus is that one or two different countries should not block the decision. Consensus should not be confused with unanimity."

> ❝ The international community works normally on a consensus basis, whether it is a regional, small organization, or a big organization. But the true meaning of consensus is that one or two different countries should not block the decision. Consensus should not be confused with unanimity. ❞

I almost think he is going to stand up and flail his arms. But this is Ban Ki-moon, not some cheap politician.

"But now just one country can block everything. One country! Look at the case of the UN Conference on Disarmament. It's only one country [Pakistan] that has been blocking progress for the last 12 years. Twelve years! They have not been able to agree on an agenda. Is that reasonable? Do we have to just accept it as a fact? That's why this year, I went to the conference and said: If you behave this way, you may lose your own prerogative, ownership, jurisdiction … This may be taken to another forum, another venue. This is just one example, only one example. How much do you expect the UN secretary general can handle all these matters? That's why yesterday's *Guardian* said, 'Don't blame him.'"

It is hard to blame Ban for saying this.

SLIPPERY DEAL SEAL

From the unique perch of the SG, Ban has carved out an inherently unique role on the global-warming front. Convinced of its reality, as identified and

> But now just one country can block everything … Look at the case of the UN Conference on Disarmament. It's only one country [Pakistan] that has been blocking progress for the last 12 years … They have not been able to agree on agenda. Is that reasonable? Do we have to just accept it as a fact?

measured by modern science, Ban has tried hard to redefine the mission of the UNSG's office for the first half of this century — as the lead international minder for shedding multi-national divisiveness and coalescing around a daunting phenomenon that obviously cannot be addressed by nation states acting alone. To many, the warming menace also defines the absolute need for the UN, or for something much like it.

The nagging scientific debate over the reality of global warming may be a genuine disagreement over facts and their proper interpretation — and not a last-ditch effort by fronts for industry and other commercial interests scared by the foreseeable costs of curbing their behavior. But Ban is not in doubt. He is convinced that the problem is real and the need for action is urgent.

I say: "Lee Kuan Yew, among many others, has said that global warming will intensify as long as the narrow national interests of nation states predominate. Are you pessimistic, too?"

Ban, soft-spoken but hard-nosed, says: "That's one area I have been feeling disappointed sometimes, but as secretary general I am advised not to say words like 'frustrated' or 'disappointed' because the secretary general can be a symbol. When he says he is frustrated and disappointed, then people may feel there is no hope."

"The risk you run is you become Jimmy Carter giving the malaise speech, and that was effectively the end of his presidency."

"And I should not do that."

"You have to almost be a naïve optimist…"

Ban laughs.

"…or at the very least a semi-naïve optimist."

"Basically I *am* an optimist."

"I know you are!"

"*Basically!*"

"No, I know you are."

Ban almost stands up at this point; he is clearly agitated: "I always think in a positive way and even with that sometimes I am disappointed, though I do not express it publicly. Then when you are dealing with global challenges like climate change and millennium development goals … and also food security and public health which threatens lives — HIV/AIDS, malaria, tuberculosis, or H1N1 like flu pandemics, and there are many unknown diseases

— those needs should be seen by all member states as a global problem and one should really act and be committed as a global leader. But they are more focused on their domestic issues. You see, they say, if we agree to this climate change deal, what will happen to us, to our economy? That is more important to them. This is disappointing and so it will be again extremely difficult. But I have been beating the drum all the time; I am the first one to bring climate change up to the top global level."

"Right, but somebody asked me about your sincerity and I said, look, I'm not an expert on Ki-moon, but what I do know about him on this issue is that he really feels it and believes it's one of those overriding issues on which the SG has a unique perch."

Ban laughs: "And I'm not the expert in climate science! But I have visited almost all the places where I could see the impact of climate change, so that I would be able to speak out with a more convincing voice. If you read and learn some information from material only from books, then your power to convince is much weaker than when you are truly convinced. My convincing power [is driven by my deep belief] and I'm going to really push this continuously."

"You probably feel you did everything you could in your first term [on global warming]. Is there anything else you can do in your second term to accelerate remedial progress?"

"Now, that's a good question. [At the start of my first term] very few people talked about climate change. The more serious leaders in the world began to pay attention, as I did."

I say I knew that. "But what are you going to do in your second term?"

Let me give you the background, he says: "Then I convened my own initiative, the 2009 climate change summit meeting in Copenhagen. Many heads of government came at my invitation to Denmark. At that time, the catchphrase was: Seal the deal. Seal the deal in Copenhagen. Everybody expected that we would seal the deal, a legally binding compliancy deal. Unfortunately, with all these member states, we were not able to do that. We made a lot of good proposals that were not accepted because member states were not ready. Then some were accepted in Cancun in 2010, some more accepted in Durban, South Africa, in December 2011. I'm very glad.

"The most important thing is that for the first time in the history of climate-change negotiation, member states agreed in Durban to sign a comprehensive, binding agreement by 2015, and then allow five more years for ratification, so that by 2020 we will have an effective treaty, a binding treaty. That was the agreement. That, I think, is the most important achievement in the history of climate change."

> I'm not the expert in climate science! But I have visited almost all the places where I could see the impact of climate change, so that I would be able to speak out with a more convincing voice … My convincing power [is driven by my deep belief] and I'm going to really push this continuously.

But will the Durban document really seal the deal, reverse the predicted trend toward a truly fearsome planet of disequilibrium?

"We agreed in Durban to operationalize this green climate fund — GCF. At this time it is an empty shell. This shell should be filled with a hundred billion by 2020 to help the developing world to mitigate the costs of adapting to this global warming impact."

This won't happen if the world economy tanks, of course. But let's stay optimistic: "So by 2020, we will have the real deal?"

"Yeah, that's right. And by that time, I will not be here, but you should remember my contribution!"

"It'll be in this book."

He laughs.

"So basically, your second-term strategy is to stay with it, keep hammering, keep pushing?"

"Yeah, sure. But we have an agreement — this is very important."

"But you feel you've got to stay with it and keep pushing?"

"Yeah, yeah, yeah."

"Will there be more Durbans, as it were?"

"Oh yes, there will be."

A Utopian Goodbye

THERE WAS A glitzy dinner in Los Angeles the night before a Hollywood stars' event called Global Creative Forum. This was a few years ago and Ban was to speak in the morning via an interview conducted as a one-on-one by Michael Douglas, the well-known actor; and then speak again that night at a star-studded dinner that included everyone from Stevie Wonder to Diane Lane to, well, Demi Moore.

Worse yet, the schedule called for him to follow Bill Clinton as speaker. That's like following Secretariat down the race track — almost anyone's worst nightmare. But Ban was actually less worried about being compared to the always talkative and sometimes eloquent former president than to Hollywood stars. He felt perhaps his own star would not shine so brightly in that stellar company…

Aides found this difficult to hear, coming from him. They felt he was so much more worthy than the fluff-balls of the U.S. movie racket. So someone explained to the UNSG how to think of his challenge the next day:

"Look at it this way, SG. When a Hollywood movie shows a scene where heads are blown off and blood is everywhere and bodies lie on the side of the street or the exploded café, and then the film's director yells 'cut', what happens? The actors get up, dust themselves off, take a shower and go home. But in the *movie* that is the UN and its secretary general, that never happens. Those bodies never get up ... to live and to act another day, much less go home. They rot by the side of the road or are buried by tearful relatives or burned by vengeful enemies. That's because they really are dead!"

The difference between his life and their life, it was explained, is that "you are real and they are not and they know it and they will be in awe of you".

Ban took all this in and considered it slowly, as is his way. He felt much was at stake in his star turn because of his hope to enlist talented and moneyed West Coast entertainment luminaries in a campaign against cynicism about the UN. He imagined documentaries and even full-length feature stories that would inspire viewers, as John Kennedy once was an inspiration for him, to see the UN from broader, more sympathetic perspectives. The UN is more than just the Tower of Babel that is often the 193-member General Assembly, or the veto-choked Security Council. It is an array of international agencies that worry over everything from malaria in Mali to preemies in Mongolia.

As it turned out, Ban's star turn went quite well.

Indeed, the eyebrows of aides in attendance at the informal dinner held in a rich man's home were raised dramatically when

Ban began his presentation by reminding the chic crowd that the "bodies at the side of the road in my life never get to shoot another scene." The celebrities got the point right away. There was a murmur of warm sympathy: *Hey, this guy is the real deal.*

"In your second term, you will have five years of experience under your belt. I mean, if you look at Bill Clinton, he was a better president in his second term than his first term. In fact, I would argue, if you could get rid of the Monica diversion, he was a very good president in his second term. He was certainly more attentive to foreign issues. You have four and a half years under your belt now. It's time for Ban to come out and swing a little bit."

"Mm. Yeah, okay."

But he doesn't seem very convinced.

"It's not that anyone wants you to be a wild and crazy guy! We don't want you to be a wild and crazy guy."

"Well, you will never see me a wild or crazy guy."

You can bet the farm as well as the nest egg on that.

"I don't mean you should go to an alternative lifestyle club with a Radiohead or something!"

He vaguely gets that. He says: "I can change a little bit."

"Nose to the grindstone, but that's Ban Ki-moon. Now, spread your wings a little … just a little?"

This is what his top advisors want him to do, including those who are the most loyal and who are convinced his 10 years will go down in history as a very good effort indeed.

Yet he returns to his view that, in the end, it is on his

performance and not his charisma that he will be judged finally. "But if I had not done it that way, I might not have been successful as a secretary general. First of all, I have had to read a lot of materials, you know, different subjects."

He is back to that.

Ban puts it this way: "Larry Summers [former Harvard president and top economist who worked in both the Clinton and Obama administrations] once compared both Presidents Clinton and Obama. He said there was a 30 percent chance that President Clinton would keep his time for a 10 o'clock White House meeting, but then 90 percent President Obama would keep time. There would be a very low possibility that President Clinton would have read his written materials for the subject he will have to chair the next day, and there'll be about 70 percent of President Obama reading all this in advance. For me, if I may say, it would be a 100 percent chance of having read all the materials without fail before I chair any meeting and 97 percent of [keeping] to the schedule. I have always been very disciplined. Now, this is one good lesson which I have given to UN staff ... discipline. They are now very quick and efficient. I did try to change their style, so I said that I will lead by example. This has been my good cause, to change the working style of the UN Secretariat — but nobody now beats me in that regard, and they do respect this. They respect."

I tell him of Clinton's remark about his reluctance to criticize a successor president in office because everyone is human and all presidents make mistakes.

"Yes, all the presidents make mistakes and likewise all the secretaries general may make mistakes. I don't claim I am a perfect person, of course. I have many weak points to be compensated by the backing of friends and supporters and member states. That's what I've been saying to our member states and journalists. Don't expect that I will be a superman. In fact, however super a man may be, without the support of member states, there is nothing I can do. This is a fact of reality of being secretary general. I'm not a national leader who has all the readily available resources — political power, military power, economic resources and money and manpower … human resources. There, all are under one disposal and jurisdiction. Here we don't have military power. I don't have any resources available, all resources and money and equipment and facilities come from member states."

> I have always been very disciplined. Now, this is one good lesson which I have given to UN staff … discipline. They are now very quick and efficient. I did try to change their style, so I said that I will lead by example. This has been my good cause, to change the working style of the UN Secretariat…

He catches his breath, reaches for a cup of tea.

"What I have is only moral power, moral authority and convening power. In that sense, this job is the most powerful for convening conferences and meetings and raising an agenda. Setting an agenda, I have that power. That's what I have been doing, I will continue to do that and I'm very strongly committed to this kind of public service. I am ready to dedicate all my life and time and energy and whatever it may be to work to achieve the major goals of the UN. That's what I have been doing and I will continue to do that."

This seems reminiscent of his thinking in the first term. It's hard to know whether his aides have told him what they truly think. It's hard to know whether he would even listen if they did. It's almost as if he believes that charisma might be some evil potion to disguise lack of substance.

One thing is for sure: Ban is Ban and nothing, for better or for worse, is going to change the Ban persona dramatically. This is Ki-moon, the eighth secretary general in history. What you see is what you get, right?

> Don't expect that I will be a superman. In fact, however super a man may be, without the support of member states, there is nothing I can do. This is a fact of reality of being secretary general. I'm not a national leader who has all the readily available resources.

Not really. Not really at all. We can see that clearly now, can't we?

It is the last time I am with Ban and Mrs. Ban for this book. We are on the second floor, hovering around the huge wooden railing over the staircase. Downstairs is the entryway and lobby. They want me to go downstairs.

But how about upstairs?

"Isn't that where the secret study is?" I say, pushily, the vulgar American journalist, nothing to lose now, the interviews all completed. And when will I see them again?

The SG glances at his wife, in the style of a silent question, as in the time we had met in the big reception room on the other side of the big stairwell.

> **What I have is only moral power, moral authority and convening power. In that sense, this job is the most powerful for convening conferences and meetings and raising an agenda. Setting an agenda, I have that power. That's what I have been doing, I will continue to do that...**

And, just as back then, Soon-taek says nothing directly. Her answer comes with body language. Without saying one word, she turns toward the other second-floor staircase, the tiny one that curves slightly wildly up to the third floor. I follow without saying a thing. The secretary general brings up the rear, maybe a little grudgingly.

The secret study is small. Two well-draped windows. A cluttered mahogany desk, not like the picture-perfect clean one on the second floor. Stacked with papers. No James Bond paraphernalia in sight, though.

Yet four points might be worth noting.

As Ban goes behind the desk to make sure nothing is showing that shouldn't be, I snap a picture or two and he scowls back a 'No'. No pictures!

But I notice the paper-shredder to his right. It is large.

I look in the other direction and notice the large bookcase. There's a picture of Ban and the Pope, among others. It is that picture which stands out, for some reason — the religious and the secular popes together.

Then the third thing I see is the cot. I had almost missed it, fully equipped for starting and ending sleep at odd hours without irritating the wife. Ah — the real secret of the secret study. It hosts the bed for the man who hardly ever sleeps.

And the fourth thing is when Ban comes out from behind the desk and gives me a gentle shove. It is the first time we have touched, other than the ritual handshake.

And I realize where he is directing me.

It is out of the study. And — in a few minutes — out of the townhouse. And — for now at least — out of his life.

Just about everything I know about him, you know now.

And, really, it's all due to the immense courtesy of Mrs. Ban. Pillow Power.

Frankly, I wish them both the greatest of luck. She deserves it, because she is good; and, as for her husband, we deserve it, for the wish to avoid the bad! All of us, all over the world, could use an SG that is both lucky and good.

Not that utopia is around the corner. In fact, utopia had better wait. Real urgent work needs to be done first. And at least we have a real hard worker at the top of the UN trying 24/7. Somehow that is a little bit comforting, don't you think?

Charisma is over-rated. Ban is a good one.

FROM DAG HAMMARSKJOLD,
UN SECRETARY GENERAL
(1953–1961) IN 1953:

"From generations of soldiers and government
officials on my father's side I inherited a belief
that no life was more satisfactory than one of
selfless service to your country —
or humanity. This service required a sacrifice
of all personal interests, but likewise the
courage to stand up unflinchingly
for your convictions."

Works Consulted
and Recommended

Baehr, Peter, and Gordenker, Leon. *The United Nations: Reality and Ideal. (4th edition).* Palgrave Macmillan. New York. 2005

Cordier, Andrew and Foote, Wilder. *The Quest for Peace: The Dag Hammarskjold Memorial Lectures.* Columbia University Press. New York and London. 1965

Cronin, Thomas, and Genovese, Michael. *Leadership Matters.* Paradigm Publishers. Boulder, Colorado. 2012

Gordenker, Leon. *The UN Secretary-General and the Maintenance of Peace.* Columbia University Press. New York and London. 1967

Hammarskjold, Dag. *Markings.* Knopf. New York. 1965

Hanhimaki, Jussi. *The United Nations: A Very Short Introduction.* Oxford University Press. Oxford, New York. 2008

Lee, Krys. *Drifting House.* Viking. New York. 2012

Mazower, Mark. *No Enchanted Palace: The End of Empire and the Ideological Origins of the United Nations.* Princeton University Press. Princeton, N.J. 2009

Mearsheimer, John. *Why Leaders Lie.* Oxford University Press. Oxford, New York. 2011

Shim, Theresa. *Korean Entrepreneurship: The Foundation of the Korean Economy.* Palgrave Macmillan. New York. 2010

Surtz, Edward, S.J. *ST. THOMAS MORE UTOPIA.* Yale University Press. New Haven. 1964

Urquhart, Brian. *Hammarskjold.* Norton Paperback. New York. 1994 (originally published in 1972)

THANKING THOSE
WHO HELPED MAKE
THIS BOOK POSSIBLE

Let me start with appreciation for my two researchers and fact-checkers of Korean-American ancestry who also transcribed many of the audiotapes. They are former students whose family-imbibed knowledge of the Korean language was invaluable. Esther Joe is now in the middle of her Master's in Development Practice at Emory University, and is projected to enter the U.S. Foreign Service before long. With all that, Esther had to hand over the researcher's job mid-course to former fellow student Yena Kim, who was also the principal fact-checker on the previous Giants book *Conversations with Thaksin*. Reading the final draft was Euna Park (in Korean, Park Yoo Na), a student at the University of California, Berkeley, who plans a career in journalism; and Lani Luo, a student columnist for Asia Media, a website at my university, Loyola Marymount. Transcribing two tapes was Erin Boone, the Utah lady who had been the principal transcriber of the prior books: No subject has complained of being misquoted yet!

Also thanking: Several aides to Secretary General Ban helped somewhat when asked, but no doubt the first among equals was Yeocheol Yoon, formerly chief appointments aide to Ban, now chief of protocol for the United Nations organization. His dedication to the UNSG is matched only by his unrelenting professionalism.

And thanking: My colleagues at Marshall Cavendish International Asia, especially the forward-thinking Publisher and General Manager Chris Newson, top Editor Mei Lin Lee and the overall editor of this book, the wise and precise Tara Dhar Hasnain. All have been a solace to me all through the ongoing *Giants of Asia* series, never letting me down. Allied with Marshall Cavendish are two book-industry pros in Asia: Leslie Lim of Pansing and Kenny Chan of Kinokuniya/ Singapore. I think of them as friends. Finally, my long-time literary agent Theron Raines, who for decades has demonstrated unerring good judgment and taste in almost everything, except very occasionally, in his clients!

About the Author

TOM PLATE, author of the ongoing *Giants of Asia* series, is an American journalist with an international career at media institutions from London to Los Angeles. Born in New York, he completed his studies at Amherst College and Princeton University's Woodrow Wilson School of Public and International Affairs, where he earned his master's degree in public and international affairs. His syndicated columns focusing on Asia and America, begun in 1996, have run in major newspapers in Asia and America.

He has received awards from the American Society of Newspaper Editors, the California Newspaper Publishers Association and the Greater Los Angeles Press Club. When he was Editor of Editorial Pages of the *Los Angeles Times*, the newspaper garnered the Pulitzer Prize for its coverage of the Los Angeles riots.

From 1994 to 2008, he taught in the communication and policy studies programs at the University of California, Los Angeles. He has been a Media Fellow at Stanford University and a fellow in Tokyo at the Japanese Foreign Press Center's annual Asia-Pacific

Media Conference. He is currently Distinguished Scholar of Asian and Pacific Studies at Loyola Marymount University, Los Angeles, as well as a Visiting Professor at United Arab Emirates University in Al Ain, UAE.

He was the founder of the non-profit Asia Pacific Media Network (APMN), whose webpage resurfaced as *AsiaMedia* at Loyola Marymount University in Los Angeles (lmu.edu/asiamedia). He also founded the Pacific Perspectives Media Center in Beverly Hills, California, a non-profit organization now under *AsiaMedia*.

On the West Coast, he is a board member of the Pacific Century Institute and a Senior Fellow at the USC Center for the Digital Future; on the East Coast he is a long-standing member of the Princeton Club of New York and the Phi Beta Kappa Society. For years he was a participant at the retreats of the World Economic Forum in Davos, Switzerland.

Professor Plate is the author of nine books, including the bestsellers *Confessions of an American Media Man* (2007), *Conversations with Lee Kuan Yew* (2010), *Conversations with Mahathir Mohamad* (2011) and *Conversations with Thaksin* (2011), all published by Marshall Cavendish Editions. Under a pseudonym, he is the author of the novel *The Only Way to Go*. He resides in Beverly Hills with his wife Andrea, a licensed clinical social worker, and their two cats.